SELF-GOVERNMENT IN
MODERNIZING NATIONS

SELF-GOVERNMENT IN
MODERNIZING NATIONS

edited by

J. Roland Pennock

PRENTICE-HALL, INC. Englewood Cliffs, N. J.

The editor wishes to express his gratitude to the following Departmental colleagues who were helpful in planning the lecture series or in making editorial suggestions in connection with the printed volume: Alan A. Altshuler (now at Cornell University), Douglas A. Chalmers (now at Rutgers University), Charles E. Gilbert, Gene D. Overstreet (now at George Washington University), David G. Smith, and Kenneth N. Waltz.

Contents

v

SELF-GOVERNMENT IN
MODERNIZING NATIONS

Introduction

J. Roland Pennock

Since the close of the Second World War, nations, or peoples, or sometimes little more than conglomerate groups of tribes, have been achieving political independence at a heretofore unheard of rate. Most of these new members of international society have just emerged from colonial status. Many of them have had no experience with self-government. Their people were impoverished, uneducated, and unused to rapid change. They were "traditional" societies, lacking both experience with the dynamism of modernity and a vision of a better way of living. With dramatic suddenness and sometimes frightening consequences, this traditionalism is giving way to an acute awareness, among the members of these societies, of the possibilities of economic, social, and political progress. They are determined to realize these possibilities with speed that could not be called "deliberate." In this determination and drive they have been joined by other states, such as Ethiopia and Thailand, not new but newly determined to modernize.

The essays in this volume are concerned primarily with the political aspects of the problems arising out of this great drive toward modernity. They were presented originally as lectures, at Swarthmore College in early 1962, under the auspices of the William J. Cooper Foundation and the Department of Political Science. In this printed version, the order has been slightly changed and the authors have made some textual revisions. No attempt has been made, however, to deal specifically with the most recent developments, for it was not the intention of the original lectures to be so descriptive or topical as to tie them to immediate circumstance.

Each of the five essayists deals with one facet of the general problem. The writers do not seek to offer final conclusions or to attain over-all unity. Three of them—Hodgkin, Pye, and Sutton—look primarily at internal problems of the developing nations, while the other two—Brzezinski and Wriggins—take a more external point of view. Two of the writers —Hodgkin and Sutton—direct their remarks largely to Africa, where they have had extensive personal experience, but most of what they say applies to the emergent nations in general.

Although the concept of "political development" (the political aspect of "modernization") has come in for considerable attention in recent years, it has yet to achieve a supporting body of theory comparable to that which characterizes its twin concept, "economic development." Perhaps one reason for this discrepancy lies in the fact that economic development —or at least most of what goes by that term—can be measured by the single and relatively simple factor of per capita income. There is no similar yardstick for political development. The economy exists to produce goods and services, which are themselves visible and measurable and reducible to a common denominator, money. The polity, on the other hand, exists to produce such items as security, justice, and liberty, which are invisible, largely unmeasurable, and not reducible to any common denominator. Political scientists of this generation, or many of them, have grown wary of dealing with such value-laden concepts. They are even wary of making the implicit value judgments entailed in ranking governments or forms of government or in speaking of political "progress." Yet "development" suggests at least a vector, with overtones of general approval or preference. And in fact political scientists working in the field of comparative politics, especially if they are dealing with rapidly developing countries, are once more finding themselves talking and writing in terms that imply valuational comparisons. At the same time they are keenly aware of the fact that political development necessarily and rightly reflects the infinite idiosyncracies of local circumstance.

The tension between the desire to apply universal standards and the obligation to allow for uniqueness is clearly felt and recognized by each of the authors of this volume. To help the reader appreciate the common frame of reference that the five contributors share, despite their varied approaches, it may be useful to call attention to how each deals with the contending forces of the universal and the parochial.

Lucian W. Pye, in the opening essay, discusses the general question of evolution or progress *versus* cultural relativism. Remarking the truth in each, especially for this subject, he shows in some detail the impact of "the modern world culture" upon indigenous cultures. Modernization entails conflict between the general and the particular. To the extent that conflict is replaced by fusion, the process of successful and orderly evolution replaces both violence and stasis. At an early stage of development, authority, even authoritarianism, is essential; but once the ground-clearing has been done, the eventually necessary fusion of the universal and the parochial can best be accomplished by the mediating activities of representative government.

Francis X. Sutton, discussing "the problem of fitness for self-government," notes that Africans now vigorously deny that this problem exists. A people, they feel, must educate themselves and work out their own destiny. Accordingly, he proceeds to discuss the subject not as a matter of "*pre*-condition" for independence, but as a matter of what conditions will enable self-government to survive. The universal *needs* for these conditions confront parochial *demands* that often conflict with them. In assessing the various forms taken by this basic conflict, Sutton deals particularly with the role played by colonialism and the reaction to it.

While Sutton's discussion emphasizes the role played, for better and for worse, by the "Western intrusion," Thomas Hodgkin calls attention particularly to the indigenous elements in the African culture. He stresses the fact that this culture has its own long and honorable history, in which the so-called Western intrusion was only an episode. Dealing largely in the realm of ideas, he points out too that insofar as Africa has

borrowed from the West it has selected revolutionary and
socialist ideas at least as often as those of classical liberalism.
Like Pye, he notes that it is really from "world culture" that
Africa has drawn ideas that it did not itself generate. Again
without using the same words, Hodgkin and Pye are together
in noting the "search for identity," both national and individual, as a vital problem confronting most of the new states.
Yet Hodgkin also feels and stresses the need for unity on a
larger front than that of the nation state. Larger political
unions, possibly complete pan-Africanism, appeal to him as
practical goals as well as useful myths.

The notion that the Marxist-Leninist version of Western thought has had perhaps a greater impact on the new
states than has Western "liberalism" is further developed by
Zbigniew Brzezinski. He shows why this body of doctrine,
which like Western liberalism claims universality, often has
more appeal to modernizing nations than does that body of
ideas which is more familiar and acceptable to most Americans. He shows also the ideological tension within world Communism and how the rival interpretations apply to the new
states. Even more significantly, he points to the tension between theory and practice within both bodies of Communist
doctrine, and suggests that the lesson of this vast discrepancy
is not wholly lost in the free lands of Asia and Africa. Perhaps
socialism is still the dominant trend—certainly an insistent
demand—in most developing countries; but parochial demands
and needs are once more asserting themselves to require
modification of universalistic doctrine and to check the easy
acceptance of foreign institutions.

In the concluding essay of the volume, W. Howard
Wriggins turns his attention to the question of guidelines for
American policy toward modernizing nations. Our scope of
action is limited by the nature of today's political environment.
Colonialism made its distinctive contributions; it also left vital
tasks to be done, certain conditions to be corrected. The emerging nations require a new order. Within the limits of its influence, the United States has an interest in facilitating and
giving direction to their political development. How? To that

simple question there is no simple answer, and no universal solution. Here is where particularity must come in. Wriggins finds middle ground between generalizations so broad as to be useless and the particularity of an *ad hoc* approach by distinguishing six types of situation and discussing the kinds of policy that are both workable and likely to be effective in each case.

Taken together these five essays on political development make a significant contribution to this urgently practical and rapidly evolving subject. Avoiding the specificity of individual country studies, they bring to bear upon the general problem of political modernization the insights of students of special areas. Without prior collaboration, the authors nontheless have brought together a series of essays that reinforce and complement one another remarkably.

Democracy, Modernization, and Nation Building

Lucian W. Pye

Few questions relating to contemporary public affairs are more puzzling, and more fundamentally disturbing, than that of whether Western political forms and ideals are appropriate or even relevant for the new states of Africa and Asia. Is it reasonable to ask impatient new states, anxious to speed up all the processes of economic and social development, to rely upon democratic institutions and procedures? What is the best way of achieving the modernization of old societies? And is there any relationship between modernization and democracy, and between democracy and nation building?

Both outside observers and those who would be the spokesmen of the underdeveloped countries have shown disturbingly little confidence as to what should be the content of political development. At what pace should a society be expected to develop competence in the management of modern institutions of government? Is there in the political realm a discernible dynamic process of national development which might serve to guide expectations about the development of particular countries? What sequence of trends can be expected in transitional societies? What are the relations between economic growth and national development? What interpretations should be placed on such tendencies as the emergence of authoritarian practices and of military rule? And finally again that most fundamental and disturbing question: Is a commitment to liberal democratic values likely to be a major handicap in nation building? Doesn't the situation call for hardheaded and singleminded leadership? The rate at which significant questions can pile up begging for answers suggests the degree to which we lack crucial knowledge about the processes of political development.

Inadequacy of Orthodox Theory

From this list of questions it is clear that intellectually the new states of the underdeveloped areas present us with a major challenge, for in a very fundamental sense the model that has emerged out of the tradition of empirical study of the American political process has been misleading when applied to most of the new states. For the American scene it is appropriate to conceive of government structures as representing the institutionalization of fundamental cultural and historical patterns of behavior, and to assume further that the dynamics of the political process consists of pressures and forces emerging from the broad social and economic bases of the country, contending with each other and striving to shape policy and influence the course of government. Thus in a sense the "inputs" of the system come from the society at large while the "outputs" are in the form of governmental policies. Changes in policy outputs alter the condition of social life and produce equilibrium adjustments until new pressures emerge calling for new policies.

In very crude terms this has been the model that has proved so useful in understanding the American political process. It is, however, unfortunately of little relevance for many of the new countries. For in these systems the source of dynamic change often resides largely within a small governing elite who control the formal structures of government, which in turn do not represent the institutionalization of indigenous cultural patterns but rather foreign importations. Thus the basic model for analysis has not been too helpful in advancing our understanding of the processes of political development and nation building.

If we turn to the field of comparative politics for intellectual guidance we still do not find much help in formulating a theory of political development. The need for new thinking and new theorizing about the problems of nation building in the former colonial world has posed questions about political development which have compelled social scientists, either implicitly or explicitly, to concern themselves anew with the extremely broad issue of trying to classify or categorize total political systems. As they have become more deeply engaged in the study of the new countries, social scientists have found increasing reasons for being dissatisfied with the simple dichotomous schemes of Western and non-Western or Modern and Traditional. We have found that it is not too helpful to lump together all the new countries in a single category since it is clear that they are often at quite different stages of development. At the same time it has been apparent that the general category of "Western" covers quite diverse systems. The total effect has been an increasing interest in arriving at typologies of all political systems, but a decline in satisfaction with a simple dichotomous scheme. The basic trend seems to be in the direction of an ever-heightening appreciation of the unique and particularistic qualities of each transitional system, a trend which has been encouraged by the very strong sense of cultural relativism basic to the outlook of the contemporary generation of American social scientists. This trend has left us in an ambivalent position: on the one hand we can readily appreciate the value of gaining a deeper understanding of each country as a separate and largely unique system, and yet on the other hand we find that if we are to talk about political development, modernization, and the encouragement of democracy we need some general principles and a means for classifying the total array of systems.

The fundamental problem at the moment is our profound uncertainty over what we should use as the general principles for differentiating and classifying political systems. The very effort of making a choice of possible classifying criteria compels us to face up to some unresolved but deeply fundamental issues in the social sciences.

The first of these is the issue of static as against dynamic analysis. The basic outlook of modern political science, which has encouraged the feeling that change is difficult, slow, and likely to occur only in incremental steps except when a system completely breaks down, has strongly biased the American social scientist in favor of seeking explanations for why things are as they are and have inhibited him from focusing on how things might be different. The problem of change has seemed to be far too closely linked to the old issues of normative philosophy and speculation about the ideal in human affairs. In short, the mood of American political scientists has been largely one of feeling that 'before we can analyze the dynamic problems of development and thus provide guidance to the new states we must learn more about why they are as they are today; but this more static form of analysis easily impresses us with all the forces which keep a society the way it is.

This problem of static and dynamic analysis is closely related to another fundamental issue in the social sciences that must be dealt with in any approach to the larger policy issue of the relations among democracy, modernization, and nation building. This is the old issue of progress and social evolution on the one hand, and cultural relativism and respect for the individuality of different social values on the other hand. The real problems of economic and political development in the new states have suddenly made us realize that we had never actually resolved the issues between the concept of social evolution and the principles of cultural relativism. We had only pushed them into the background. We realize now that we have been living with both; at some moments we have been cultural relativists and at other times we have found it more convenient to talk in terms of evolution, growth, stages of development, and other such concepts inherent in the view of social progress.

The dilemma posed by the issue of evolution *versus* cultural relativism is made more acute by the ability of the economists to rank different countries according to indices of relative development which suggest an essentially unilinear concept of progress. If we can so readily speak of stages of economic development, why shouldn't we be able to do the same with political development? Indeed, as we learn more about the dynamics of economic development it becomes increasingly apparent that the conditions of economic growth are closely linked to cultural attitudes and political practices, and hence economic development cannot be independent of political and cultural development.

Once the problem, however, is pushed to this point, we are confronted with the issue of what should be taken as the criteria of political development. And once these issues of values are raised the pull of cultural relativism becomes overpowering. Who is to say what state of social affairs is more advanced or more retarded? And we are quickly back to all the doubts about the appropriateness of applying concepts of progress, development, and modernization to the political sphere.

The clash between evolutionary theory and cultural relativism is a basic one and cannot be easily sidestepped. At the same time, however, it does seem possible to recognize that to a considerable degree we can surmount the difficulty if we alter the historical and analytical perspectives from which we customarily approach the problems of political development.

The issue of evolution *versus* cultural relativism is most acute when we think in terms of a world composed of more or less autonomous political systems. Unfortunately this has been the fundamental outlook basic to most contemporary social science. In comparative politics, for example, we have tended to analyze countries as though they were relatively isolated and independent political systems with their own inner dynamics. Once the problem of change is posed in these terms we are compelled to search for law-like propositions which might describe the change, "growth," and "development" of such systems. At the same time we also are compelled from this approach to respect the unique configurations of each particular system. It is therefore precisely a consequence of our thinking of societies as relatively autonomous systems that we are confronted with the frustrating issue of the search for evolutionary "laws" and the appreciation of cultural uniqueness.

The historical facts suggest, however, that change is generally not a problem basic to separate and relatively autonomous systems, but rather that it is overwhelmingly related to interactions among systems. Social change can in many ways be generated by isolated social systems, but the historical set of major changes which we are concerned about when speaking of the problems of the new states is clearly a function of cultural diffusion. In particular when we treat the problems of nation building it is not appropriate to think of a world of autonomous systems each developing, growing, and maturing according to some fundamental laws of organic change and evolution. Nation building in the present age is taking place in a world in which powerful international currents are pushing the various societies in roughly the same direction.

It is useful at this point to quote at some length the anthropologist Robert H. Lowie at the conclusion of his classic study of social organization, *Primitive Society:*[1]

The belief in social progress was a natural accompaniment of the belief in historical laws, especially when tinged with the evolutionary optimism of the 'seventies of the nineteenth century. If inherent necessity urges all societies along a fixed path, metaphysicians may still dispute whether the underlying force be divine or diabolic, but there can at least be no doubt as to which community is retarded and which accelerated in its movement toward the appointed goal. But no such necessity or design appears from the study of culture history. Cultures develop mainly through the borrowings due to chance contact. Our own civilization is even more largely than the rest a complex of borrowed traits. The singular order of events by which it has come into being provides no schedule for the itinerary of alien cultures. Hence the specious plea that a given people must pass through such or such a stage in *our* history before attaining this or that destination can no longer be sustained.

Lowie reminds us also of the profound words of the jurist Maitland in *Domesday Book and Beyond,* which he quotes:

> Even had our anthropologists at their command material that would justify them in prescribing that every independent portion of mankind must, if it is to move at all, move through one fated series of stages which may be designated as Stage A, Stage B, Stage C, and so forth, we still should have to face the fact that the rapidly progressive groups have been just those which have not been independent, which have not worked out their own salvation, but have appropriated alien ideas and have thus been enabled, for anything that we can tell, to leap from Stage A to Stage X without passing through any intermediate stages. Our Anglo-Saxon ancestors did not arrive at the alphabet or at the Nicene Creed by traversing a long series of "stages"; they leapt to the one and to the other.[2]

It does seem possible that the present-day tensions of international politics, the spectacular material success of the industrial societies, and the ever-increasing pressures of expanding populations in backward countries may be combining to create a special historical and temporal form of "inherent necessity" which Lowie did not feel at his time of writing but which has become a powerful force in contemporary world politics. This form of "necessity" which can appear only in the form of political demands and pressures does not change the inherent nature of societies nor does it justify our thinking of societies as being governed by specific and universal laws of growth. Indeed, there is considerable danger that in the light of the pressing policy problems of development in the new states people will come to think increasingly of all human societies as organic entities with very definite patterns of growth. This is especially likely to be the case as we tend more and more to apply shorthand terminology to different ranges of policy problems and thus to speak of country A as being at such and such a stage of development and country B at another stage. If we are to use such terminology we must constantly remind ourselves that we have no solid intellectual grounds to justify the notion that all societies must or are likely to pass through discernible and historically progressive stages of evolution.

It is true that many respected philosophers of history and students of civilization have postulated that societies have life cycles which follow discernible laws. Basic to the thinking of such different men as Marx, Toynbee, and Spengler has been a common effort to elucidate the sequences of growth, development, and decline of human societies. And certainly the founders of modern sociology were intensely interested in the problem of social evolution. Max Weber, in seeking to explain the industrial revolution in Europe, formulated the evolutionary patterns of changes in forms of authority in which the traditional system gave way to the charismatic, and then, if development continued, the rational-legal form of authority would emerge.[3] Auguste Comte also formulated a three-stage progression of social evolution: the theological, the metaphysical, and the positivist periods.[4] And of course many others have sought to find some historical order in the experiences of societies and civilizations. For our purposes it is not necessary to evaluate all of these efforts; it is sufficient to recognize that these authors have been dealing with units of human history that are far larger both in terms of cultural areas and historical time than the relatively modest units represented by the new states of the underdeveloped areas. Whatever the merits of any particular theory about the rise and fall of civilization, they are not likely to be manifest when applied to the situation in the various new states of the contemporary underdeveloped world.

Nation Building and a World Culture

In turning our backs upon the possibility of discovering any set of laws that might govern recognizable stages of development we are not necessarily driven to the conclusion that there is no order or pattern behind the direction of

change in the underdeveloped areas. The theoretical nature of
our problem changes fundamentally when we recognize that
the present-day question of political development in the new
states is directly connected to an historical epoch, and that
therefore our search should not be for universal laws about
the ultimate direction of social development but rather for a
clearer understanding of how the contemporary forces at
work in the world are likely to affect the particular experiences of the currently underdeveloped countries. For we are
now witnessing a massive diffusion of culture.

When the European world first pressed outward and
learned of the worlds of Africa and Asia there was some basis
of mutuality in the contacts. It would have been hard at the
time of these first contacts to have predicted how the inter-
change of cultural contacts would have affected each side.
But at an ever-accelerating rate the direction and the volume
of cross-cultural influences has become nearly a uniform pattern of the Western industrial world imposing its practices,
standards, techniques, and values upon the non-Western world.

This massive flow of cultural diffusion is most clearly
manifest in the political realm. The development of the nation-
state is only in part an autonomous, domestic process, for all
states are shaped in very fundamental ways by the fact that
they are units of a nation-state system, and they are constantly
called upon to interact with that system. Indeed, the nation-
state has little meaning in isolation, and most of the concepts
basic to the operations and organization of the modern nation-
state are derived from the standards common to the international community of states. Starting from the problems of
defense and foreign policy and carrying over into the fields
of membership in the United Nations and the control of international trade and commerce and on into the realm of the
domestic management of affairs, a host of very explicit pressures move governments in certain very definite directions.

Although the particular institutional forms of government, and the organization of the polity, and the spirit of the
political culture all may vary within wide limits, there are

certain minimum qualifications of statehood in the international community which place demands upon the development of all nation-states. These demands go beyond just those related to the functional needs of the nation-state system as a whole and reflect what we might call the cultural climate of that system. That is to say that there is also what we may call a "world" or a "cosmopolitan" culture which is closely related to the nation-state system.

We cannot dwell here on the content of the world culture; it is sufficient to observe that it does have a degree of inner coherence, and it is generally recognized as being the essence of modern life. It is based upon a secular rather than a sacred view of human relations, a rational outlook, an acceptance of the substance and spirit of the scientific approach, a vigorous application of an expanding technology, an industrialized organization of production, and a generally humanistic and popularistic set of values for political life.

Once we recognize the demands and the attractions of both the nation-state system and the world culture we can begin to appreciate the basic stresses that must underlie the nation-building process in the new states. We can now see why our initial questions as to the relevance of what we first called Western institutions to the underdeveloped countries are inescapable. Up to a point all societies must adjust to the historical facts of our era, and they must adapt their economies, societies, and polities to the world system and the world culture. Thus we can see that the underdeveloped countries are sharply limited by their own historical experiences in being introduced into the world community and by their continuing need to preserve their identity and sovereignty in the world community of states.

All of this is to say that there is a minimum level of what were once Western but are now world standards which the new states must accept if they are to survive in a world of independent nation-states. Thus the international political and cultural fashions of the day set the general direction of development for the new states.

The Process of Acculturation
to the Modern World

Since there is a great variety of ways in which separate
societies may be acculturated to the world systems and the
world culture, the problems of nation building are directly
related to the dynamics of the acculturation process, and not
to any form of natural evolution or organic change in autonomous systems.

Those features of the acculturation process which are
peculiar to each non-Western society are generally related to
the characteristics of their particular traditional cultures and
the conditions under which they were exposed to the West.
In some societies the traditional order represented great civilizations with elaborate patterns of social relations; in others
it consisted of relatively primitive peasant communities with
no written traditions. Since each type has its distinctive basis
for response to the Western impact, the task of analyzing the
process of modernization becomes one of distinguishing how
different types of traditional societies have reacted to contacts
with different dimensions of what we have called the world
culture and which, historically, chiefly involved contacts with
European culture. We can readily distinguish different patterns of acculturation which may largely determine the course
of nation building.

First, there were differences in the *auspices* under
which Western influences were introduced. In some instances
it was traceable primarily to the activities of private Western
individuals and organizations; in others the agent was Western rule in the form of colonialism; in still others the Western impact was mediated through an indigenous elite.

Second, there are the differences in the *spheres of life*
most immediately affected by Western influences. Colonialism
operated directly at the level of government. Other forms of
Western influence primarily affected commerce, education, or
religion.

Third, there have been great differences in the *intensity* and the *direction* of the Western impact. Some traditional societies have been exposed to the West over long periods of time, but the intensity of the exposure has been relatively low. In others the Western challenge has been an intense one over only a brief span.

Fourth, there are differences in the degree of *violence* which accompanied the most intensive Western impacts. In Southeast Asia the more gradual and less violent process of change was suddenly and abruptly altered by the Second World War and the period of Japanese occupation. Elsewhere non-Western societies have been spared the more violent impacts of the modern world.[5]

The manner in which these different elements of the acculturation process are combined in any particular case produces the different patterns of the diffusion of modern culture. In every case there is a considerable element of the unique and the distinctive; and yet there are also certain fairly general patterns: the former colonial territories which shared a common European ruling power, the countries of the same traditional cultural area, or, for example, those countries with the same kind of economic activities and industries. In every case, however, it is possible to ask whether the process of acculturation has produced a fusion of the old and the new or whether the result has been a fragmenting of the society.

In a sense, fusion is the process which produces a new culture and a new society which will still be unique but which will incorporate organically elements of the modern world culture. The particular form of fusion will determine the level of economic and technological advancement of the new culture and the structures and effectiveness of its social and political institutions.

If the acculturation process produces fragmentation, that is, the old and new elements are not being adequately integrated, the very order and coherence of the exposed society may be seriously threatened. Changes in the society may be extensive or quite limited, but the important fact is that with fragmentation the political system is unable to manage the process of change.

At the heart of the acculturation process in all transitional societies lies an inherent conflict between the need for order and the need for continuing change. The diffusion of the world culture is fundamentally disruptive of all traditional forms of social organization. At the same time, however, the process of diffusion demands that societies maintain the necessary degree of order so as to prevent the disruption of the international system and of those domestic systems essential for supporting aspects of the world culture.

Bases of Political Stability and Instability

The state of equilibrium between order and change is thus critical in determining the political condition in any transitional society at any particular moment.

In this context we would note first that the essence of political stability is that it is a requirement for the realization of directed and purposeful change, since stability connotes a public policy which effectively reflects and satisfies the changing scheme of values within a society. In direct contrast, political instability connotes a public policy either too rigid and inflexible to accommodate the changing balance of values in the society or too vacillating and unsure to be able to advance any objectives. Thus political stability can be associated with change that is rationally directed toward satisfying the social needs of the maximum possible proportion of the population, while instability is associated with change that fails to gratify the social demands of the people and leaves an increasing proportion frustrated.

Second, we would note that the dynamic factor in creating tension has generally been the uneven and discontinuous process of social change in the direction of greater urbanization, for it seems that in transitional societies the rate of urban growth has far outstripped the rate of industrial and economic development which is the functional basis of the modern city. People have chosen the life of the city even when they cannot find there the functions usually associated with a modern city, a development which demonstrates that individuals can become acculturated to a modern way of life far more readily than societies can be reorganized.

The connection between the general principle of the relationship between political stability and social change and the fact of uneven and discontinuous social change in the transitional societies is demonstrated clearly by the case of the highly trained Asian who finds that he cannot apply his new knowledge and skills in his underdeveloped society. It is similarly demonstrated by the less educated person who has turned to the city in search of a more exciting and richer life and who cannot find activities to which he can hitch his ambitions. It is plain that when institutional development lags behind the pace of individual acculturation the grounds are created for serious personal frustrations.

The great difference between the pace at which individuals can be acculturated to the modern world and that at which societies can be reconstructed is the source of the great human tragedy of the underdeveloped areas. In such circumstances human resources must constantly go to waste or be grossly misapplied. The cycle of ambition and frustration also opens the way to profound insecurities and a subsequent decline in effectiveness and competence. People who have been disappointed too often cannot be effective agents for the great and demanding tasks of nation building.

When we look beyond the individual we see that most transitional societies lack two of the essential prerequisites for a stable system of representative government. The first is a social mechanism whereby it becomes possible to determine and clarify continuously the pattern of values and interests within the society and relate these to the pattern of power through an aggregating and bargaining process. The second is the availability of appropriate instruments for carrying out public policy once the society has expressed its relative values and interests—that is, an efficient bureaucracy which

is not just one of the dominant political groupings in the
society.

Although the lack of these prerequisites in a transitional society constitutes a basic weakness, it is possible for
the society to avoid excessive tensions if those who have political aspirations can be recruited into the elite society and
accept its outlook. Indeed, some such form of political tutelage
is essential if a traditional society is to adopt a more modern
form of political life. The danger always exists, however, that
the current elite will strive to maintain its administrative and
political monopoly and not permit the development of the autonomous roles of the administrator and the politician. When
this occurs, the resulting rise in authoritarianism is reinforced
by the fact that the elite is becoming even more isolated from
the masses.

The failure of most transitional societies to develop
those who can skillfully articulate the values of the population
creates other dangers. Even if it advances programs that con-
form to the broad aspirations of the population, no government can harness the energies of the people unless there is
genuine communication between the decision-makers and the
population. If the public is to be identified with the programs
of the administrators, the people must have a sense of participation in the making of the decisions which most directly
affect them. Although the elite can assume the initiative and
dominate the communication system, some mechanisms for
determining and expressing mass attitudes are essential if the
energies of the society are to be effectively mobilized.

The lack of those who can perform the full role of the
politician is also a major reason why the gap between aspiration and reality becomes a source of general frustration in
many transitional societies. An important but often overlooked
function of open and competitive political articulation is that
of creating in the minds of the public a better appreciation of
the distinction between the plausible and the possible.

In societies experiencing rapid cultural change people
are often just beginning to learn that they can change their
condition of life through political effort. Since people en-

grossed in the problems of acculturation tend to stress the forms or styles of behavior, their behavior is guided by their images of an ideal and ultimately desired way of life and not by the realities of the existing situation. They feel that it is no longer appropriate to be restrained by the essentially cautious and shrewd outlook on life common to traditional and peasant societies, but they find it difficult to determine what should be the new and realistic standards for guiding their behavior.

In transitional societies large politically significant elements of the population feel that they can expect a new relation to exist between effort and reward but are still unsure as to what this relation actually is. They tend either to believe in pie-in-the-sky promises or to distrust completely the words of the politician. Hence the role of the articulating and competing politicians becomes important, since it is through exposure to their messages that a public can develop a sense of political realism without losing an appreciation for the appropriate function of idealism. In time the public can learn that in listening to political discourse it is necessary to discriminate between the exaggerated language that constitutes the wrappings of political promises and the actual policy implications that are partially hidden within the messages.

To summarize and to return to our attempt to identify the central cause of political instability in transitional societies, we would point to the lack of an effective relation between the ruling elites and their peoples. We see that in some instances political instability is directly connected with the fact that sudden and sharp changes in intra-elite relations are possible because the key members of the elite do not have any firm commitments to the interests of particular segments of the public and so are free to act according to their personal interpretations of what is advantageous in the limited sphere of intra-elite relations. Consequently their behavior often tends to be essentially opportunistic. We see that in other instances the elite may remain united but project to the public only its own views of what is socially and politically desirable. Even though they may believe themselves to be sympathetic to the aspirations of the people they may be in fact isolated in their own world. It is clear that when for any reason the gap between elite and public is excessive there is both opportunity and temptation for any set of would-be leaders, with or without valid qualifications, to attempt to fill it—a situation almost inevitably fatal to hopes for political stability.

Democracy and the Fusion of the Universal and the Parochial

We may return now to our original questions about the applicability of Western institutions, and particularly of democratic practices, for the process of nation building in the new states. It should be apparent from our analysis that we are dealing with a problem that is on the one hand deeply grounded in the context of our particular period of history, but which on the other hand is of such tremendous significance for the development of world history that it does seem to constitute a universal problem, above all particularistic considerations of time and place.

The fundamental problem of nation building at this stage of history in most of the new states is that of finding a satisfactory reconciliation between the universalistic dimensions of the world culture and the parochial expressions of the local culture. A modern nation-state represents not only the political applications of all the technologies, attitudes, and knowledge basic to what we have called the world culture but also a unique expression of the local and special interests of a distinctive community of people. The essence of nation building in the new states is the search for a new sense of collective identity for an entire people—a sense of identity which will be built around a command of all the potentialities inherent in the universal and cosmopolitan culture of the modern world, and a full expression of self-respect for all that is distinctive in one's own heritage.

During the first stages when the world culture is being introduced into a transitional society, the process can be greatly facilitated by the application of authoritarian means. Indeed, it is possible to establish much of the infrastructure of a modern state through such imposed methods. Of course colonialism performed this function in many of the new states. Yet the very inadequacies of colonialism as a modernization agent point to the limitations of authoritarian methods in the building of modern states.

More precisely there appear to be three inherent limitations of authoritarian methods in introducing the world culture. First, harsh and apparently unfriendly agents of acculturation may strengthen a people's feeling that the world culture is essentially foreign and hence a threat to the self. The result may be psychological counterreactions and a subsequent rejection of the new imposed patterns. Second, authoritarian methods often increase the tendencies toward fragmentation rather than toward fusion. Acculturation is likely to occur only in limited spheres, and sharp divisions may later appear between those so acculturated and those who have not been so directly acculturated. Finally, authoritarian methods appear to be of value only in creating the role of the administrator and hence of formal government, and not in strengthening the role of the politician and hence of the political process. Consequently, excessively authoritarian methods in first introducing the elements of the world culture can produce a profound imbalance between government and politics, impeding complete nation building.

At a second stage of nation building the need is for bringing together the universal and the parochial. This stage requires a more intimate relation between the government and the masses. This is the delicate stage when the particularistic sentiments and the real interests of the people must be brought into the political process without disrupting the requirements of the state apparatus. The merging of the cosmopolitan and the parochial can appear to be done through populist movements and enunciation of nationalist ideologies, but in the main these turn out to be synthetic attempts. For only rarely in human history has it been possible for a creative individual to give expression to the sense of identity of an entire people, and under conditions of rapid social change this is particularly difficult.

The attempts of African leaders to give expression to the "soul of Africa," to find the "African personality," and to identify themselves with the "spirit of Pan-Africanism" reflects this urgent need to bring together the universal and the parochial. Yet often these attempts seem to fail in giving a genuine sense of identity to the emerging polity because what is claimed to be the parochial does not in fact represent specific and concrete interests within the society.

It is at this point that the basic functions of representative government become critical in the nation-building process. If these new societies are going to achieve a new level of integration, they must find methods for giving representation to both cosmopolitan and parochial forces. Out of the interplay of representative politics it is possible for a society to realize a fundamental fusion of elements of the world culture and the indigenous traditions. This is because competitive politics forces people to classify their real interests, to seek a rational relationship between ends and means in their social life, and to distinguish between the realms of private and public policies—precisely the problem of identity which often plagues people in transitional societies. With competitive politics both individuals and a society can fuse elements of the modern cosmopolitan world with their own historic sense of individuality. This process of blending lies at the heart of the modernization process; and it is this fact which justifies our faith that there is a close association between democratization and modernization.

Notes

1. Robert H. Lowie, *Primitive Society* (originally published in 1920 by Horace Liveright; reprinted by Harper Torchbooks, New York, 1961), pp. 440–41.
2. *Ibid.*, p. 435.
3. Max Weber, *The Theory of Social and Economic Organization*, trans. by A. M. Henderson and Talcott Parsons (Glencoe, Ill.: The Free Press, 1947).

4. Auguste Comte, *The Positive Philosophy*, trans. by Harriet Martineau (London: George Bell and Sons, 1896).

5. This discussion follows the line of analysis of the character of non-Western societies and their exposure to the West in George McT. Kahin, Guy J. Pauker, and Lucian W. Pye, "Comparative Politics of Non-Western Countries," *American Political Science Review*, Vol. XLIV, No. 4 (December 1955), 1022–41.

The Problem of Fitness
for Self-Government

Francis X. Sutton

Mandates under the League of Nations, trusteeships under the United Nations, and the policies of all the colonial powers have assumed that there were places and peoples not yet rightfully ready to govern themselves. Once there were independent African states, this whole doctrine was called into question. It was boldly assaulted by those early and radical leaders of African independence, Kwame Nkrumah and Sekou Touré, who proclaimed that their own independence in Ghana and Guinea was imperfect and incomplete as long as other parts of Africa remained under colonial rule. Nkrumah's famous slogan, "Seek ye first the political kingdom," subordinates the problem of fitness. So, more radically, does the demand for immediate and general African freedom—a demand that has not been merely Soviet propaganda or "Casablanca" radicalism but was presented, for example, by President Yameogo of Upper Volta at the "summit conference" in Lagos of January 1962. Thus a doctrine still enshrined in United Nations policy has been categorically rejected by leaders in the part of the world that has been most substantially affected by it. To suggest that self-government may be denied to peoples and areas because they lack conditions deemed essential to self-government is now to risk moral condemnation.

The problem, however, persists. If peoples may claim categorically the right to venture self-government, they still must meet certain conditions if they are to continue in effective exercise of self-government. There are unfortunate examples in the present world of countries large parts of which are not controlled effectively by their governments. They lack the essential minimum of cohesion or integration on which effective government can be based. In other cases, the stability of government is so precarious that continuity of policy or even the elementary keeping of order is seriously impaired. Obviously there may be substantial differences in the meaning of effective self-government for a territory or a nation. Occasionally, one has heard radically consistent African politicians (like Mr. Oginga Odinga of Kenya) declaring that Africans should be free to do as pessimistic Europeans have proclaimed they would and revert to tribalism. If the right to self-government meant simply the right to organize social life and government in a territory in any way it pleased the inhabitants (or some ruling minority of them), then discussion of the conditions of fitness for self-government would ascend into the thin generalities that describe the functioning and coherence of any society. The problem can be made more concrete and determinate, of course, by taking the conditions that have imbued trusteeship concepts. Other ways of giving it more particular content can also be conceived. But it is not necessary to have recourse to idealistic or purely scientific definitions. There is in fact in the world today a very general and common agreement on what modern self-government means.

Whatever the poverty, backwardness, or remoteness of a nation today, it must be trying to be modern and prosperous, not just existing comfortably or fatalistically in its own present condition. Neutralist politics do not insulate new states from the examples of the developed nations. Citizens and governments in the new nations seek policies and practices that will, in some finite time, make their countries into modern developed ones. If some reasonable chance of progress toward this goal is taken as a condition of fitness for self-government, then hope is restored that we may be able to say with some concreteness when a nation is fit.

Any effective government depends on common bonds or loyalties that stretch across tribes, classes, or ethnic groups and make a people or peoples into a nation. The kind of gov-

ernment required for a developing nation is a definite species
of social structure that has its own special conditions.

It belongs to a genus that sociologists, following Mac-
Iver, usually call "associations." These "associations" are so
familiar a part of the structure of developed societies that
unless we are sociologists we are more conscious of their
variety than of a basic similarity in their structure. Business
firms, hospitals, universities, governments, and a great variety
of other organizations share common characteristics in their
functionally specific purposes and their operation on universalistic principles. Social structures of this general type are
rare or absent in most of the societies the world has known,
and without them the levels of performance that make developed societies are hardly possible. Thus the task of development is very largely the construction of associations. One
basic requirement is that there be trained people who can
fill the occupations that are the building blocks in these associations. This is the "manpower" aspect of development which
is nowadays rightly receiving great attention. Without people
competent to act as executives, administrators, professional
men, clerks, or skilled workers, a nation cannot operate a
modern state or make much progress toward doing so. Given
qualified people, one may perhaps hope in time to put them
together into well-functioning governments, business firms,
and other organizations. But this does not happen automati-
cally and the task of putting together these organizations is
more than a simple "manpower" problem.

To see whether a modern nation is fitted for self-government we thus should look at its underlying social cohesion,
its trained manpower, and its equipment in modern associations.

One might, no doubt, take more general and analytical
approaches, but it seems to me promising to look at a group of
new nations in their concrete historical setting, hoping thereby
to view the problem of fitness in realistic but not too severe
terms. Because my own acquaintance with the new nations is
best in Africa I shall concentrate on that continent. There the
relevant historical setting is that of imperialism and the West-

ern control it brought for a period of about 75 years over prac-
tically all of the continent. It was during this period of Western dominance that the conditions must have been laid for
present fitness for self-government, and we must look back
to the colonial era to understand the form and urgency that
problems now take. There are of course respects in which
Africa differs from other continents, but it shares a history
of Western domination with the great majority of new states
in the world today, and a suitable analysis of the African nations from this starting point may take us considerable distance in understanding new nations wherever they are.

The Beginning of New Nations
under Western Domination

Broadly speaking, the effect of Western domination
was to impose a new elite and in many cases a completely new
form and extent of political integration on previously existing
societies. With rare exceptions, existing political authorities
were degraded in importance and dignity or completely over-
thrown. If they persisted, it was made apparent that a greater
power than they was in being. The effects of this affront to
indigenous political leadership were likely to be pervasive: A
king losing the aura of majesty undermined those sentiments,
religious and secular, that his dignity had expressed and en-
forced.

The gap between the culture of the intruding Europeans and the cultures of most people in the non-Western
world was sufficiently great that close intermingling did not
readily occur. There was a tendency for the powerful, Western
elite to become something like a closed caste. Economists have
spoken of a dual economy in many of these countries. I think
it proper to speak more broadly of "dual societies." The elite
Western community was never completely insulated from the
society in which it lived but social distinction, separate institutions, and ecological fact went far to separate it from the
mass of the indigenous society in which it lived. What has now

become hateful anachronism in the Apartheid of South Africa was in fact quite normal on the African continent. Europeans and Africans lived separately, not only in Johannesburg and Salisbury, but in Leopoldville,[1] Nairobi, and even in Lagos and Accra. So it was in North Africa as well. One finds it already a little improbable that the Avenue Bourguiba in the middle of Tunis was, not very long ago, no place for Tunisians to live. Deferential etiquette and differences in style of life went with this physical separation, reducing and regulating the social intercourse that could go on across the caste-like barrier.

Obviously, this situation made no ideal school for "backward" peoples. Their prospects of winning control of their own societies and governing them in a modern sense depended on chances of learning from the alien elite, and this required contact of many sorts.

The penetration of Western influences in non-Western societies has depended very broadly on the thoroughness of political control, and on the extent and form of economic development. In the past, empires have characteristically left major portions of the areas they controlled relatively untouched. We know, for example, that outside the cities in Asia Minor, the Romans left age-old village structures intact. Something of the same sort of uneven impact may be seen in the era of modern imperialism. But the influences of government and the world economy have reached very far. In Africa, for example, while vast rural areas have persisted in illiteracy and subsistence agriculture, they are not as they were before. The authority of the administrator, the desire of missionaries to convert the heathen, opportunities for wage labor and the astonishingly extensive migrations it has provoked have all deeply affected parts of the continent that outwardly keep primitive forms.

Western intrusion meant not only the coming of Westerners but their institutions as well. The indigenous peoples came into close contact with these institutions and participated in them. From the point of view of the Westerners, this was a matter of practical economic necessity. In government, in industrial, commercial, and agricultural enterprises, an effort was typically made to utilize the indigenous people as a labor force. Boys were trained to be clerks in Khartoum, Dakar, or Leopoldville. They came from all over central Africa to the mines of Katanga and Northern Rhodesia; and they crowded more and more into the towns of the continent, giving them a spectacular growth in recent years. (Abidjan grew from 20,000 to 119,000 in the years between 1933 and 1955; Leopoldville from 36,000 to about 350,000 between 1938 and 1959; and Dar es Salaam from 23,000 to 125,000 between the years 1931 and 1959.) Despite the insulating etiquette of these dual societies, urbanization brought a whole series of diffuse contacts between Europeans and Africans within and beyond the contexts of everyday work, and these contacts became more and more telling as Africans ceased to be migrant workers and settled down with their families in the towns. The close imitation of a well-observed European elite that occurred has been abundantly documented by sociologists.[2] This urbanization has been especially important because the Europeans in Africa have been so typically urban dwellers. Germaine Tillion has pointed out the separation of European and Moslem populations that lay behind the Algerian tragedy, with the European population very thin in the countryside and living overwhelming in large and small cities "as much as possible among themselves."[3] South of the Sahara, it has been estimated that 75 percent of the European population has been urban.[4]

These varied opportunities helped many Africans to acquire the habits and values displayed by Europeans, but they did not readily lead to a full range of experience in modern organizations. Lack of educational qualifications was one basic reason. It was characteristic of these African dual societies that while a primary education was available to a fair number of Africans, opportunities to go on to secondary and higher education were very few until the years after World War II. Any notion that Africans should have opportunities for education that would equip them for the professional and executive roles in modern societies was slow to emerge. Poli-

cies differed in different places, and it is notable that among
African examples, the British West African territories stand
out as ones in which there was relative abundance of educational opportunity for Africans. It was precisely these territories in which the concept of temporary British responsibility for countries which were ultimately to be African was
most clear. Where what may be called "true colonialism" has
prevailed, i.e., territories in which it was thought possible for
Westerners to have a permanent place as elite citizens if not
necessarily as sole tenants of political power, African educational opportunities have been relatively few. Thus for example
in Algeria in 1954, there were 200,000 European men and 1,-
600,000 Moslems aged between 20 and 50. Of these, among the
Europeans, 180,000 men had been to primary school and 30,000
to secondary school; among the Moslems, only 100,000 had
been to primary school, and 3,000 to secondary school.[5] Similarly in Kenya, there has been compulsory education for European children to age 15 since 1942, while as late as 1960 only
30 percent of the Africans went beyond four years of primary
school and only 12 percent on from the intermediate school
to secondary education.[6] Historically, the earliest opportunities for education beyond the elementary level in many countries came most abundantly under the stimulation from the
needs of the missions. These were of two sorts: the need for
teachers in elementary schools, which led to the growth of
teachers colleges, and the need for an educated African clergy.
The remarkable prominence of former school teachers and ex-
seminary students among the present leaders of Africa is thus
explained.

I have dwelt a little on this matter of educational opportunity because of its evident importance in equipping nations with the manpower necessary for self-government. It
has, no doubt, a special importance in Africa, but it is, I believe, crucial elsewhere, too.

A review of occupational opportunities during the colonial era would reveal a profile somewhat similar to that of
educational opportunities—a fairly broad base, but not much
at the top until the very end of the era. The tardy development

of organizations run by Africans throughout their levels follows as a logical consequence. To review these questions empirically would take much space, and I must try a quicker course through a general analysis of the effects of the dual society that existed under colonialism.

The management of a colonial society by a minority elite rested upon sureness in the authority of this elite. A white man in Africa had to be sure of deference and obedience simply because he was a white man. Maintenance of his position by continued use of force was not at all practicable. Force might be used upon occasion to punish transgressions or to give dramatic demonstration that challenge to the white man's authority would not be tolerated. But the basic dependence had to be on respect and deference accorded to the ruling minority as such. The extraordinary peace and security which prevailed over most of Africa after the initial conquests is evidence of the success that was attained. A kind of public order, which independent states now have cause to look upon with suppressed envy, was achieved. A powerful elite, perched on top of diverse tribal and ethnic groups, insensitive to their inter-African differences, and requiring that all respect the European's peace, made possible movements and interrelations of African peoples that had previously been impossible. Dahomeyans could teach in half the elementary schools of the Ivory Coast or run the postal services of Senegal. Educated Ibos could be the clerks of an expatriate government in Northern Nigeria, shielded from the contempt and hostility of Fulani and Hausa. The growth of towns mixed peoples of different customs and origins, and the habits of submission to a colonial territorial government began to give some consciousness of unity among the diverse inhabitants of the territory. Perhaps most important, the European elite bred a new African elite. The Africans who learned the ways and the competences of the Europeans gradually became an elite in their own societies, overtopping and displacing traditional African elite. This new elite had more than local status, and common experiences made it a unified African elite that could ultimately take control of a unified territory. Wrestling now with tribal

and other fissures in their own independent states, African
leaders give stinging denunciations of the colonialists who are
allegedly responsible. But the argument is a very thin one, and
the legacy of unity, peculiar though it was and built on social
discrimination and authoritarian control, is a real contribution of colonialism toward the social integration the new
states need.

   The pattern of European elite and African mass worked
less aupiciously as a school for Africa organizational competence and responsibility. In a pattern of this sort, it was
possible for Africans to reach positions of respect and authority only if they had exceptional qualifications. They had to
demonstrate beyond question their technical or professional
competence, and show moreover that they had assimilated at
least the essential cultural characteristics of the ruling elite.
In a post-Enlightenment world, none of the colonial powers in
Africa was quite prepared to take a straightforwardly racist
line. In principle social ascent was possible. But the conditions, given the nature of the dual society as I have depicted it,
were made especially severe. If ambiguity existed, then the
rightness of the white man's rule would be questioned. It was
in keeping with this logic that the categories of *évolué* and
assimilado came into the nomenclature of African colonial
policy and that admission to them was so notoriously slow and
difficult. It has latterly been the charge of African nationalists
that the pioneers of African advancement became "black Europeans." This seems quite justified; to be such was an essential condition of their acceptance by the controlling Europeans.

   Not only were standards placed conservatively high.
Behaving in the way Africans were expected to behave had an
inhibiting effect on their advancement. By having to assume
deferentially submissive positions African experience was
impoverished and self-confidence impaired, while Europeans
were confirmed in their indispensability as guides and super-
visors. This aspect of the human relations of colonialism has
not yet had anything like the amount of serious analysis it
deserves. The most enlightening discussion I know is Man-

noni's, based on his long experience of Madagascar.[7] His notion is that the sort of relationship psychologists and in particular psychoanalysts describe as *dependency* has been widely characteristic of the adjustment indigenous peoples assumed vis-à-vis European rulers and superiors. A relationship of this sort is not simply one of submission to the more powerful. There are qualities of acceptance, warmth, and loyalty in it, and it holds gratifications for both partners that make the relationship hard to break. Such a view makes colonialism something better than brutal oppression, but it leaves it a poor matrix for developing the autonomous personalities needed to man the social structures of the modern world. It is only too evident that many Europeans in Africa came to believe in a slow political evolution because they were comfortably convinced that Africans would need paternalistic guidance for a long time. People who "knew Africa" from long experience were often less the champions of African advancement than people at home in the West who viewed the problem with more detachment and easier response to moral principle.

During the latest period—particularly after World War II—it became a more and more widely accepted policy that the control of colonial powers was to be a temporary one, and should properly be a trusteeship in which African peoples would benefit from a tutelage that would bring them well equipped to self-government and independence. Given the facts of social relationships as I have described them, it would be surprising if this process of tutelage could have been carried out smoothly and in good time. It has not been, and hence much of the interest and urgency of the problems here under discussion.

Anticolonial Reactions and Political Precocity

The argument I am here presenting shares with Marxism a quality of pathos. While it does not say, as Marxism does, that some rationally perceived or intuitively felt eco-

nomic interest made a smooth dissolution of colonial power
impossible, it suggests other reasons why that process could
not be carried out when all was well prepared and time was
ripe.

The forces which have brought independence were long
latent in the colonial situation. They became politically effective when development had gone far enough to permit direct
assault on alien control. Frustration, resentment, and hostile
reactions there had always been. The submissive, dependent
reactions I have described were real, but not all of the story.
After the shock of conquest and in the early stages of colonialism, reactions to frustration and misery took obliquely rebel-
lious or otherworldly forms. Africa has had a rich assortment
of separatist, so-called Ethiopian, churches and apocalyptic
movements (like that faraway offshoot of Jehovah's Wit-
nesses, known as the Kitawala, in the heart of the Congo and
in Northern Rhodesia). The solidarity of Africans against the
dominant whites marked all these movements. Once it became
possible for leading Africans to make a plausible challenge to
European *political* control in the Europeans' own terms, they
could turn this solidarity into a base for claims of popular
representation with which no European could readily compete.
This possibility came when relatively small numbers had acquired the secondary or higher education which equipped them
for effective negotiation and disputation with Europeans. So
equipped, they became plausible representatives to their people and the spokesmen of popular democracy and self-determi-
nation to the Europeans.

Thus the movement to political independence rested on
a popular solidarity that did not pay direct regard to questions
of competence or the state of development of national populations. In the kind of tutelage which the more responsible colonial governments attempted to manage, there was the fatal
difficulty that those who stood as the alien elite were the
judges of competence and readiness for advancement. At a
certain point, Africans came to dispute these judges and hence
to obstruct an agreed evolution. There was a hope among responsible colonialists that educated, "evolved" Africans might

become their natural allies in a controlled movement to what they regarded as well-prepared independence. This hope was defeated by the sociological facts that I have stressed. No matter how successful an African might be in climbing over educational hurdles and winning occupational competitions, he remained an African, conscious of a castelike separation from Europeans. He was thus little disposed to resist movements that spoke in the name of all Africans, regardless of their attainments. Once the tide was running toward African political solidarity, he would risk isolation and charges of betrayal if he agreed with cautions voiced by Europeans.

African independence has thus come with a strong populist flavor. It has been an assertion of the rights of common men more than a confident claim of maturity. As I pointed out at the outset, dwelling on questions of fitness for independence has taken on a quality of impropriety. At best, the subject is blurred by sensitivities and controversy. The colonial powers worriedly protest unreadiness, while the insurgent nationalists indignantly reject open or implied charges of their incompetence. If the foregoing analysis has any merit, one may perhaps without partisan commitment speak of a precocious political development that brings many states into being very uncertainly equipped to manage their own affairs. To say this is not, of course, to challenge the moral rightness of the process. But it does confirm that fitness of these new nations for self-government may be an urgent problem.

The Internal Cohesion of New Nations

The new nations in Africa have started with the governmental apparatus that was left to them by the colonial powers. Independence meant not a deliberate dismantling of governmental institutions, but mostly a change in the people who occupied places in them. With a kind of social and political inertia the old machine could run on into independence, strong in its accustomed authority and routines. Of course, its very different base would show effects in time, but there are reasons for its lasting that have often been underestimated.

Much has been said about the artificiality of modern African states. But despite oratorical torrents on African unity, the lines drawn on the map during the colonial scramble show few signs of being washed out. The African solidarity that brought independence was a solidarity within the bounds of existing territories. The experience of common effort in the independence movement made African masses conscious of being Nigerians, or *Ivoiriens,* or Tanganyikans and bound them together as they had not been before. I have emphasized that independence movements typically have had their leadership drawn from the new, educated African elite, and there has been strong pressure to include all of the elite of a territory in one unified movement. Unity has been in considerable measure achieved, and African states have emerged with their political institutions staffed and supported by their most widely respected people. A basic condition for political stability has thus been met.

But we know that there have been abundant difficulties, with lurid examples in the tribal strife of the Congo or Rwanda, and dark predictions of what may happen in Kenya and elsewhere. Behind the well-known and spectacular examples, there lies a fearsome tangle of conflict and hostilities that seems to stir with new agitation after independence. I recall, for example, the Dahomeyans mentioned above. These people who, because of early educational advantages, had spread over most of French-speaking Africa are now being driven home or made so insecure that they depart voluntarily when they can. Everywhere, local people press their claims against outsiders who had been secure under the colonial regime.

The root of these difficulties appears to lie in the fact that removing the alien colonial elite from the top of African societies upset the whole pattern of social integration that had existed under colonialism. People who had been bound together in common submission now pull apart. They do so not merely because constraints are gone. I have said that African nationalism is a populist movement claiming rights for Africans regardless of their distinction or station. This permissive doctrine opens the way for the local and special interests of diverse communities and peoples that make up any typical African state. Tribal, ethnic, and local ties remaining strong, they have a new potential once they can gain legitimate expression. Their demands cannot readily be resisted by leaders who feel their duty and strength to lie in representing all the people. Sekou Touré has gone so far as to remind educated Africans that they must humbly regard themselves as more corrupted by alien influences than ignorant African peasants. When such values prevail, the capacity of an elite to foster national unity is obviously threatened, and politics become invaded by what Clifford Geertz calls the "primordial sentiments."

A ready antidote to these internal differences after independence lies in the enthusiastic unity that brought independence. There is consequently a tendency to look to a party or a national leader to resolve conflicts and preserve unity. The totalitarian implications of such dependency are obvious, and there are many indications that these implications are real. But dangers of this sort are not the dangers of anarchy, and the emphasis on political unity can make a base for effective self-government, *provided* that there is executive strength to support policy.

The boundary between administrative problems and political problems is never very clear and it becomes peculiarly hazy in the new states. What may appear as unmanageable lack of social cohesion would in the face of a stronger and more efficient governmental machine be quite manageable; and conversely, administrative feebleness may raise political storms that would otherwise never occur. The preparation of African states in trained manpower and competent organizations is thus intimately linked to the balance of centrifugal and centripetal forces I have been discussing, and all must be summed up together in assessing the fitness of these states for self-government.

Manpower and Organization in
the New States

The success of national independence movements in
Africa has resulted in a typical situation where independent
governments are not fully staffed by nationals from their own
territory. There is, of course, great variation. In the Northern
Region of Nigeria, for example, more than a year after independence there were 670 British civil servants still in the administrative and technical services of that government.[8] In
the Eastern Region of Nigeria, the administrative services
were virtually Nigerianized by the time of independence in
1960, although in the technical services only some 40 percent
of the officers serving in the higher grades were Nigerian.[9]
Ghana in the same year and after three years of independence
showed a picture somewhat similar to Eastern Nigeria, with
only 31 out of 1,680 governmental administrative posts still
in the hands of expatriates, while in various categories of
technical service substantial percentages of expatriates were
still to be found (almost three-quarters of the engineers employed in Ghana in 1960 were expatriates).[10] In some of the
African territories that were formerly colonies of France,
large numbers of French civil servants have continued after
independence. An estimate for the Ivory Coast in 1961 was
1,200, and approximately the same number were still in Senegal
at the same time. In other cases independence brought abrupt
departures of large numbers of civil servants with no ready
African replacements at hand. This was the notorious and
unfortunate experience in Guinea; it was also true in the
better prepared but seriously affected Sudan in 1956. The best
known case of an ill-prepared independence is of course that
of the former Belgian Congo. That country had only about 20
university graduates at the time of independence and hardly
any Congolese were experienced in high-level governmental
responsibility.

Numerous manpower studies have now been made in

Africa, covering employment in private business as well as in government. They characteristically show large gaps in African control of the higher administrative and professional positions. The conclusion is evident that if fitness for independence is measured in terms of effective administrative and professional control of government and the national economy, most of the African states have come to independence unfit. But this need not necessarily be the conclusion.

It is in fact clear that the negotiations which brought independence were typically carried through with the assumption that there would be continued service to African governments by Europeans who had served the colonial governments, and by others who would come to fill gaps as needed. The educated African elites have wanted to make effective modern states and they have, in general, appreciated the indispensability of good administration. Similarly, the colonial powers desired to maintain political and economic relationships which assumed that there would be modern standards of administration in African countries. The familiar conception of neutral public services made it plausible that Europeans could serve African masters and numerous arrangements were made to facilitate their doing so. In cases such as the Belgian Congo, it was patently the assumption of the retiring colonial power that quite massive European participation in the independent African government and its economy would be possible.

There has not yet been time for full testing of the assumption that independent African states would continue to accept and use foreigners in their governments and economies. But the evidence thus far suggests that expectations have been unduly optimistic. African governments have been losing their European staff faster than seemed likely, and in many cases before Africans are prepared to replace them. The places vacated by retiring Europeans can often be filled by Africans through very rapid advancement, but this results in a dangerous thinning of experience, as, for example, is noted in a report on the Eastern Nigerian government by my colleague Dr. J. D. Kingsley:

Colonial civil servants of long experience and broad administrative background have been replaced for the most part by young Nigerians fresh from a university or with, at most, a few years of experience in teaching or in a commercial establishment. . . . The average member of the Administrative Class entered the public service in the summer of 1956: roughly three and a half years ago. Only 13 officers in the entire administration have been in government as long as ten years. . . .

Length of service in a particular post has naturally been even shorter. Half of the administrative officers have served less than two years in their present position and only 19 in the entire administration have served in their present capacities as long as five years: a period of time often suggested as that required to master the elements of a complex administrative job.[11]

In this case as in others, there has not been simply a need for new faces to replace old ones in a stable organizational structure. The political changes attending self-government and independence have produced considerable institutional fluidity. Kingsley further remarks,

The difficulties of the administration have been multiplied by the pace and scope of constitutional and structural changes in the last five years. Regional self-government was quickly followed by the creation of new institutions of local government, by the redistribution of powers and functions between local and central governments, by the institution of Ministerial Government and the consequent integration of departments into ministries. Any one of these changes (and I have listed here only a few of the major ones) would have presented a sufficient challenge to a long established administration. Under the circumstances, it is altogether remarkable that chaos did not result and that the affairs of government were successfully carried on.[12]

For reasons I have set forth above, the effects of these rapid changes in African governments are hotly controversial.

I have, for example, been told by a minister of one of the African governments experiencing the greatest suddenness of departure of colonial civil servants that no significant disruption of the public services was caused thereby; he assured me that the greater part of the work had in reality been done by African subordinates and they simply took over the dignity and privileges that previously had been denied them. On the other hand, in another African state I recall the judgment of a foreign technician that the affairs of that government after a year or so of management by its own nationals were in such chaos that they were mercifully ignorant of their bankrupt situation. Typical reality lies somewhere between these illustrations of prejudice. We are unlikely ever to have a precise scientific assessment of the quality of functioning of African organizations in this early postindependence period, given the extreme sensitivity of the question, but it is necessary to my theme to attempt some general remarks.

There is no doubt that symptomatic difficulties are very common indeed. The principal ones, noted by both Africans and outsiders, are perhaps: (1) slowness, (2) lack of initiative, (3) a tendency for decisions to be pushed up to excessively high level, (4) corruption, and (5) authoritarian arbitrariness. Enumeration of these symptoms will bring vivid examples to the mind of anyone recently acquainted with the functioning of African government—of competent senior officials groaning under the weight of things they must attend to personally, of letters unanswered, decisions postponed, and personal interests improperly intruding. A fair and balanced discussion of the meaning and causes of these symptons would take a long time. African organizations have no monopoly on them, but it is plausible that they take pronounced forms there because of lack of experience, lack of technical qualification, and the difficulties of new people working together. I have given reasons for the view that African independence came and European professionals and administrators departed before enough Africans were trained to levels that had been characteristic for the positions that needed to be filled. This alone would make ample difficulties. But there is also the fur-

ther problem of shifting modern organizations out of their
original colonial matrix into an African one.

The administrations that preceded self-government and
independence in Africa had national characteristics of their
colonial authors—British, French or Belgian executives and
professionals controlled the organizations and set their tone.
The sense of authority, competence, and responsibility which
these officers had was based on a common cultural background
and their cooperative effort was facilitated by this common
background. The forms of transition that were envisaged by
responsible colonial administrators assumed that Africans
would gradually acquire values and attitudes comparable to
those held by Europeans themselves. In a limited number of
cases the results have been striking; outstanding African administrators in the former British territories of Africa behave
remarkably like their British tutors; and they have counter-
parts among African *fonctionnaires* whose excellent French is
only the most evident result of long and deep immersion in
French methods and ideas. But for reasons set forth above, not
enough of these men were trained for long enough. A great
many of the people now in positions of responsibility in Africa
have gotten there quickly on a basis of limited training, while
remaining deeply involved in traditional African societies.

One of the most popular themes of African discussion
nowadays is the potential of characteristically African qualities for aiding African development. There are unquestionably
qualities found in some African traditional societies—like ac-
tivism, pragmatism, and cooperativeness—which may be of
great value in the tasks now being faced. On the other hand, it
is obvious that traditional African societies do not make a
good match with modern industrial and governmental organizations in patterns of authority, interpersonal relationships,
and criteria of reward. It is a familiar point that many actions
perceived as corruption by Europeans are no more than the
discharge of diffuse responsibilities to relatives, friends, and
dependents in African society. Similarly, the diffuse respect
and authority commonly given to superiors in traditional
African contexts contrasts with the peculiar limitations of

authority in bureaucratic office. If we add to these disparities the recollection that to take over a modern bureaucracy means imitating an erstwhile European elite without betraying African solidarity, we have a sense of the heroic burdens many Africans are now undertaking.[13]

A rapidly and completely Africanized government is thus likely to have serious difficulties in functioning both because of the inexperience of the people in it and the necessarily rapid shift in the character of the government. There is clearly a problem of bridging over from a government of European character to the new creation that a distinctively African and modern government must be. It seems that things would go best if a rather gradual Africanization could occur. But as I have suggested, the facts are that change is not gradual. Why the pace of Africanization and the departure of Europeans should be so lively is a subject that deserves a lengthy analysis in itself, and I only venture the remark that the demands of national cohesion often seem to accelerate the pace of change and hence bring damage to executive competence. Stressing national solidarity in contemporary Africa means stressing the solidarity that brought independence, and this was directed against Europeans. It involves assertions of African competence too, with effects that are unsettling to the delicate business of retaining foreign administrators and specialists.

This is all rather gloomy. I have deliberately made it so by addressing myself to the problems rather than the advantages of independence or the constructive steps that are being taken to meet its problems. A great deal that is heartening could be said. Astute and responsible leaders who understand these problems are not lacking. They have in the political loyalty of their people an instrument for coping with national problems that no previous colonial government, however experienced and accomplished, could have. They have aroused concern and solicitous attention in the outside world as a source of help. The specific problems of fitness that I have emphasized are appreciated by governments which are now

assiduously planning to meet them. The manpower problems
in particular are being realistically faced. A recent report on
post-secondary education in Nigeria is now justly famous
and its principles limitated; this "Ashby Report" for the first
time laid out clearly and realistically what an African country
must do if it is to gear its educational system to providing
the African manpower for a progressive modern state running its own affairs. At a meeting of Ministers of Education of
the African states at Addis Ababa in May, 1961, it was agreed
that manpower planning units should be established in all
African governments, and there has been substantial progress
toward carrying out this resolution. One might almost say
that manpower development has become a tenet in the latest
version of African nationalist ideology.

But when all the proper compensations and correctives
have been applied, the equipment of the new African states
for self-government in progressive conditions looks precarious
at the start. I hope I have given a persuasive explanation why
this should almost inevitably be the case. Generous and far-
sighted colonial statesmen on the one side and strong African
leaders on the other have made some states better prepared
than others. There are important differences of degree, but it
would be foolish Utopianism to believe that the genius of the
Lyauteys, Guggisbergs, and Eboués might have been multiplied to arrest or divert a historical movement of this magni-
tude and interlocked complexity and make the outcome radically different. We now have a problem of weakly equipped
new states because of an era of colonialism and imperialism;
the colonial societies of this era produced nationalistic aspirations faster than their masters expected or could plan to gratify them. Swift and deep social changes marked the whole
process which leaders and statesmen could only struggle to
control as best they might.

Precarious readiness for self-government at the start
means the likelihood of slumps and disappointments. Governments burdened with the responsibility not only to keep the
peace but to make their countries rise in the universally de-

manded course of economic and social development are given little time to weather the changes of independence and thrust ahead. There is already ample evidence that the early years of African independence will not be easy ones and perhaps the critical problem facing that continent now is to weather these rough years while building during them for a later spurt with better trained people, more practiced organizations, and a more settled national unity.

The prospects for democracy in these early postindependence years are certainly not bright. The difficulties of unity being as great as they are, and the experience of democratic institutions so slight,[14] the overwhelming disposition is to sacrifice political diversity for the security and the supposed effectiveness of unity. It can be argued that this is a prudent choice. But it also seems clear that radical crushing of democratic institutions can be a barrier to development both in the short and long run. Some of the reasons lie in the alienation of the scanty supply of well-trained manpower and damage to the links to the developed world from which qualified specialists must be sought. The future of African democracy may depend on the conviction of African leaders that considerations of this sort deserve weight and that the fastest course to wealth and power need not be through a grim totalitarian discipline.

My discussion of this problem of fitness for self-government has been largely confined to the areas I have seen and dare think I know a little. Conclusions drawn from African experience certainly need modification to fit different conditions elsewhere, but I should hope that the broad lines of this discussion are not grossly inapplicable to those nations that have been under colonial domination elsewhere. These, as I remarked earlier, are most of the cases. The nations that preserved their independence throughout the invasion of the world by the West undoubtedly require a different treatment, hopefully not so difficult as to defy an ultimate synthesis. I look forward to the day when some bold and brilliant fellow will put it all together for us.

Notes

1. I have hardly seen any more dramatic representation of falling of colonial barriers than some maps which show how Africans spread after July 1960 out of the areas to which they had been confined in Leopoldville, to squat in areas that had previously been reserved for Europeans or for uses other than housing. (In unpublished research by Paul Raymaekers, Institut de Recherches Economiques et Sociales, Lovanium University, Leopoldville.)

2. See, for example, the report on Stanleyville in the UNESCO volume, *Social Implications of Industrialization and Urbanization in Africa South of the Sahara,* 1960.

3. Germaine Tillion, *Les Ennemis Complementaires* (Paris: Les Editions de Minuit, 1960), p. 113.

4. United Nations, *Report on the World Social Situation,* 1957, p. 144.

5. Cf. Tillion, *op. cit.,* pp. 115–16.

6. Colony and Protectorate of Kenya, *Education Department Triennial Survey 1958–60* (Nairobi, 1961), pp. 25, 27.

7. O. Mannoni, *Psychologie de la colonisation* (Paris, 1950), translated into English by Pamela Powesland under the title *Prospero and Caliban* (New York: Praeger, 1956), with an interesting foreword by Philip Mason.

8. J. D. Kingsley and Sir Arthur Rucker, "Staffing and Development of the Public Service of Northern Nigeria," January 1961, Appendix, Table I, pp. 1 and 3.

9. J. D. Kingsley, "Staff Development in the Eastern Nigerian Public Service," Official Document No. 7 of 1961 (Government Printer Enugu, Eastern Nigeria), p. 5.

10. "Survey of High Level Manpower in Ghana, 1960" (Accra: Government Printer, 1961), p. 20.

11. J. D. Kingsley, *op. cit.,* p. 5.

12. *Ibid.,* p. 6.

13. One illustration of these problems that is familiar to me through the work of the Ford Foundation is in the government of the Western Region of Nigeria. This government is unquestionably among the best run and most effective of present-day African governments. It is largely in the hands of the Yoruba people of Western Nigeria, a society in which there has been a strong tradition of hierarchical authority both within kin groups and in wider political organization. Diagnostic and training programs in that government have indicated certain characteristic problems of communication and initiative. Effective administration has seemed to be hampered by a tendency among subordinates to be more concerned to discern the attitude of someone addressing information or instructions to them than to note precisely what is being said. This anxious attention to whether the other person approves or disapproves, likes or dislikes, one is readily understandable against a background of hierarchical relations in the African society. Similarly, the diffuse authority and prestige of

high-placed Yoruba have seemed to inhibit personal initiative among subordinates. The seriousness of these problems to Africans in this and other African public services has been suggested by the enthusiasm with which courses and workshops in human relations have been received. These exercises, which are almost wearisomely familiar in the training of Americans in business and public administration, seem to be excitingly new to Africans. They provide an outlet for accumulated frustrations and appear to give a sense of new power in coping with the demands of new positions. These experiences have been discussed by Donald Nylen and J. Robert Mitchell in a multilithed report, "Staff Development and Human Relations Training" (The Ford Foundation, Lagos, Nigeria, 1961).

14. See my paper, "Authority and Authoritarianism in the New African States," *Journal of International Affairs*, Vol. XV, No. 1 (1961).

The Relevance of "Western" Ideas for the New African States

Thomas L. Hodgkin

I must admit at the outset that I am somewhat dissatisfied by what seems to be the accepted method (in Western Europe and North America) of discussing questions of the type suggested by the title of this article: questions, that is, involving in some way or other the relationship between the terms "Western ideas" (or "values") on the one hand and "African" (or "new," or "developing") "states" (or "nations") on the other. The difficulties seem to arise partly from a confusion about what is meant by Western ideas, partly from a misunderstanding, or misinterpretation, of the political processes taking place in modern African states, and partly from the lack of an adequate frame of historical reference. This statement may sound a little sweeping. The remainder of this essay is, in large part, an attempt to amplify and justify it. If the approach seems somewhat negative and critical, I can only say, like John Locke, " 'Tis Ambition enough to be employed as an Under-Labourer in clearing Ground a little, and removing some of the Rubbish that stands in the Way to Knowledge."

The Variety of "Western" Influence

Let us consider, first, the conventional view of the transfer of "Western ideas" to African societies, as it is presented by those who, on balance, approve, and by those who disapprove, of the process and its consequences. Here are two contrasting accounts: the first by Mrs. Elspeth Huxley, who belongs to the latter, disapproving, category,

> . . . Our [British] universities are full of eager [African] students preparing to return with the principles of democracy, trade unions, superannuation, logical positivism and nitrogenous fertilisers packed into their brief-cases and, with any luck, a junior Ministership awaiting them at the other end. They are the agents of the new, the cultural colonialism, which liberals are as anxious to propagate as ever 19th-century Tories were to spread their colonialism of soldiers and profits. . . .[1]

The second by Professor Edward Shils, who describes the situation in more sympathetic terms,

> . . . Africans are attached to the better sides of the West because it embodies values to which they have become profoundly attached—personal liberty, privacy, a chance to take a critical attitude towards things, a chance to make one's own individual way, a chance to enjoy some more sophisticated pleasures in personal relationships and in culture. . . .[2]

Both Mrs. Huxley and Professor Shils, you will notice, when discussing the transfer and impact of Western ideas, seem to restrict the term "Western" to one particular subsystem of ideas—those associated with "liberalism" or "liberal democracy" (however these may be defined). But this surely will not do. If one is concerned with the influence of Western ideas on African societies, one must take into account the Western tradition of social and political thought in its entirety, not simply select some particular aspect of it or theme within it. Marx, Bukunin, Sorel, Pareto belong to this tradition, as much as Locke, Voltaire, or John Stuart Mill. Proletarian democracy is a Western concept as much as parliamentary democracy. Indeed the Marxist branch of this Western tradition is clearly of special significance in a number of modern African states. The antirationalist, elitist, and racist conceptions which became embodied in the ideologies of Fascism and

Nazism are also, in another sense, Western ideas, which have
had their impact on African societies. Hence "Western" in its
popular, contemporary—and, one hopes, transient—Cold War
sense should not be confused with "Western" in the more
fundamental sense of the whole body of thinking about the
problems of society and political organization which had its
origins roughly twenty-four centuries ago in the eastern
Mediterranean, and whose influence has during the last two
centuries come to be diffused throughout the inhabited world.[3]

This is not simply a matter of language. I am not just
saying "Please, in future, for 'Western ideas' substitute 'liberal
ideas.'" Indeed, it is, I am sure, the impact of *Western* ideas,
in the widest sense of the term, on African societies that we
ought to think about, not merely the impact of *liberal* ideas. In
the course of their history the peoples of the African continent
—particularly, but not exclusively, those social groups which
at different times constituted their elites—have been exposed
to various aspects of what I have called the Western tradition
of political thought. It is worth remembering that, so far as
West Africa was concerned, the source from which this Western tradition was first introduced was not our Western Europe, but the Maghrib—the Arab West. By the fourteenth
century, I think one could safely say, certain Aristotelian
concepts, embedded in Islamic moral, political, and legal theory, had penetrated into the Western and Central Sudan.[4] A
tradition of Islamic scholasticism, not totally unlike the tradition of Christian scholasticism in medieval Europe, based on
centers of learning such as Timbuktu and Jenne, was well
established by the fifteenth and sixteenth centuries. Hence
when Commander Clapperton, the first representative from
Western Europe to visit the Sokoto Empire, encountered Sultan Muhammad Bello, who had been brought up in this Islamic-
scholastic tradition, in 1824, he confessed that he was unable
to hold his own with him in theological disputation.[5]

By the end of the fifteenth century those in contact
with the earliest Portuguese settlements along the West African coast began to be acquainted with medieval Christian the-
ology, connected by another route with the Platonic-Aristote-

lian tradition.[6] This particular Western influence was, no
doubt, extremely restricted in range—except, perhaps, in the
old kingdom of the Congo. But it must be remembered that
there are large areas of modern Africa—the former Belgian
Congo and the territories under Portuguese rule are obvious
examples—where the medieval Christian view of society and
social relations, adapted (or distorted) to meet the requirements of the colonial epoch, has been the dominant form in
which Western ideas have been officially presented to Africans. The theory that men are "naturally" unequal; that it is
"natural"—and therefore right—for society to be hierarchically ordered; that it is right for the irrational many, lacking
the capacity for independent moral and political judgment, to
submit themselves to the authority of the rational few—this is
clearly a theory that is very relevant to the colonial situation
and can be used to justify the authoritarian institutions imposed upon an African society by a European administrative,
commercial, and ecclesiastical ruling class.[7]

Of course, Africans have been confronted with many
versions of the Western authoritarian, elitist theory of the
state, of which the modernized medieval-Christian version is
only one. In South Africa they have had, and have still, to deal
with a peculiarly repulsive racist distortion of Calvinist doc-
trines.[8] British empire-builders of the generation of Lugard
and Harry Johnston (in his earlier years), more interested as
a rule in the practical problems of colonialism than in its presuppositions, tended to combine Tory paternalism, belief in
the *Gentleman-Ideal*, with a Social-Darwinist attitude to history.[9] These modes of political thinking, expressed in various
patterns of colonial institutions, and in the attitudes of the
European ruling classes, were what Western ideas most commonly meant to Africans *in Africa* during the period from the
close of the nineteenth century to the end of the Second World
War—and, in many African territories, until a much more
recent date.[10] These were Western ideas as actually experienced. It was in reaction to ideas of this type, as I shall try to
show in more detail later, that the early movements of anticolonial revolt and protest, and at a later stage the nascent

national movements, began to construct their own distinctive ideologies—whether revolutionary or reformist, expressed in religious or in secular language.[11] And a literature of protest, expressing these reactions, developed—whose general character can be illustrated by the following short extract from the writings of the late David Diop, a Senegalese poet:

> *Le Blanc a tué mon père*
> *Mon père était fier*
> *Le Blanc a violé ma mère*
> *Ma mère était belle*
> *Le Blanc a courbé mon frère sous le soleil des routes*
> *Mon frère était fort*
> *Le Blanc a tourné vers moi*
> *Ses mains rouges de sang*
>   *Noir*
> *Et de sa voix de Maître:*
> *"Hé boy, un berger, une serviette, de l'eau!"* [12]

It is, however, also true that, from the end of the eighteenth century, a limited number of Africans, established in Europe or the Americas (for the most part as a consequence of the slave trade), came into contact with this other aspect of Western political thought, "the ideas of European liberalism" (in Harold Laski's sense of the term).[13] But here again it is important to be careful about meanings. The "liberal ideas" in which the intellectuals among the Africans of the Diaspora of the late eighteenth and early nineteenth centuries seem, to judge from their writings, to have been especially interested were, fairly naturally, not the "liberal ideas" that are generally approved in this present age of NATO and the Congress for Cultural Freedom: parliamentary government, two- or multi-party systems, an independent judiciary, a "nonpolitical" civil service, toleration of (non-Communist) minorities, and the like. They were interested in what was doubtless a vaguer—but at the same time a more passionate, more revolutionary—formulation of "liberalism": the idea that "all men are brothers"; that God created men equal, with equal rights to "life, liberty and happiness"; that peoples have an inalienable right to choose their own governors and to "cashier them for misconduct"; that man is "perfectible," and humanity capable of achieving unlimited progress in the arts of living.[14] An interesting early example of the influence of this type of political outlook (which in these days it is perhaps less confusing to call "revolutionary-democratic" rather than "liberal") and its application by an African to the African situation occurs in a work by Ottobah Cugoano of Ajumaku (in what is now Ghana), published two years before the French Revolution:

> Those people annually brought away from Guinea are born as free, and are brought up with as great a predilection for their own country, freedom and liberty, as the sons and daughters of fair Britain. Their free subjects are trained up to a kind of military service, not so much by the desire of the chiefs as by their own voluntary inclination. It is looked upon as the greatest respect they can show to their king, to stand up for his and their own defence in time of need. Their different chieftains, which bear a reliance on the great chief, or king, exercise a kind of government something like that feudal institution which prevailed some time in Scotland. In this respect, though the common people are free, they often suffer by the villainy of their different chieftains, and by the wars and feuds which happen among them. . . . Nevertheless their freedom and rights are as dear to them as those privileges are to other people. And it may be said that freedom, and the liberty of enjoying their own privileges, burns with as much zeal and fervour in the breast of an Aethiopian, as in the breast of any inhabitant on the globe.[15]

Exaggerations of African Borrowing from the West

So far I have merely tried to give some content to this very general term "Western ideas," to indicate the diversity of its meanings. But I am even more worried about the prob-

lems involved in discussing the *relationship* of these ideas to
the contemporary African situation. How do those ideas which
we choose to label "Western"—and, more particularly, ideas
associated with the liberal, revolutionary-democratic, and
Marxist traditions—become "relevant" for modern Africans?

We are all familiar with the conventional way in which
this process is commonly described by Westerners. We are
presented with the image of the young Nigerian, *Malien,* or
Tanganyikan, who leaves his "tribal" environment and proceeds to Harvard, the Sorbonne, or the London School of Economics, where he reads Mill's *Essay on Liberty,* Rousseau's
Contrat Social, Engels' *Anti-Dühring,* and other exciting
works of this kind; enjoys some measure of civil liberties, and,
on the whole, equal relationships with "white" men—and
women. After a few years of student life in a Western university, back he goes to Nigeria, Mali, or Tanganyika, where—
thanks to his experience of "our" higher education and "our"
political and social institutions—he becomes sharply aware
that life under a colonial regime, or in a "tribal" society, is
not life as Mill, Rousseau, or Engels thought it should be lived.
Moreover, European officials refuse him jobs and fail to invite
him to afternoon tea. Much distressed, he becomes a nationalist leader and rouses the masses with the aid of principles
borrowed (in varying proportions) from Mill, Rousseau, and
Engels. The masses follow him (why is seldom made clear);
political concessions are granted; the colonial government
totters; the ex-student, with his associates, takes over power.

I have, I admit, somewhat guyed this stereotype. But
accounts of the revolutionary processes taking place in modern
Africa not much less rudimentary and misleading have appeared, and continue to appear, in the West, and still seem to
be taken seriously by their authors and their readers. Hence
one feels bound to ask what is wrong with this approach.

First, even if one confines oneself to considering the
personal histories of university-educated members of the national leadership (and their importance can be much exaggerated—in many African territories they played a negligible
part during the formative period, from 1945 to 1960), even

then what actually occurs is much more complex than this type of account would suggest.[16] The Western political classics have naturally had some influence on the development of the opinions and outlooks of African nationalist leaders during their student days. Indeed, some of these leaders have helpfully included samples of their reading-lists in their published works. Dr. Kwame Nkrumah has told us how, while a student in the United States, he read Hegel, Marx, Engels, Lenin, Mazzini, and Marcus Garvey—and was most strongly impressed by the last.[17] Dr. Nnamdi Azikiwe, in his *Political Blueprint of Nigeria*—published early in 1944, and providing in a sense the ideological basis for the National Council of Nigeria and the Cameroons, formed later that year—quotes Aristotle, Thomas Aquinas, Locke, Montesquieu, Rousseau, Bentham, Mill, and Bryce in his explanation of the meaning of "democracy" in the Nigerian context.[18] But in practice the channels through which ideas have flowed have been many and various: the writings of Gandhi and Nehru, Mao Tsetung and Aimé Césaire; the *New Statesman* and *Temps Modernes;* the conferences and committees of student organizations—FEANF, UGEMA, WASU; the *Présence Africaine* network; the dormitories of Lincoln University, the cellars and teashops of Bloomsbury and Holborn, the cafés of the VIᵉ *arrondissement*. African students, like students all over the world, have worked out their interpretations of "democracy," "freedom," "national liberation," "Socialism," "Pan-Africanism," and the like, primarily through discussions with their contemporaries: with other Africans, with West Indians, Arabs, Indians, Chinese, Vietnamese, Georgians, Uzbeks—representatives of peoples who had the opportunity to start somewhat earlier on the process of national and social revolution —as much as with Englishmen, Frenchmen, or Americans. This being so, I am doubtful whether it any longer makes sense to attach this label "Western" to ideas that belong to the liberal, revolutionary-democratic, or Marxist traditions: ideas that have a common European origin, certainly, but have become in this century universal—the concern of humanity, not the private property of "the West." [19]

This stereotype is based on another, more serious, misunderstanding. It implies that the process described—whereby African political leaders take over, reinterpret, and apply to the problems of their own society, concepts which have been evolved in some other social context—is a process of a special, unusual, and even somewhat improper, kind.[20] But in fact it is simply an example of a process of cultural borrowing which has constantly occurred throughout human history. We are familiar with the fact that the Arabs, in order to develop their theological and philosophical systems, drew heavily on the Greek tradition, and particularly upon Aristotle, just as later the theologians and philosophers of medieval Europe drew heavily on Ibn Sina and Ibn Rushd. The *philosophes* of eighteenth-century France owed a good deal to John Locke, and modern English and American logicians owe, I believe, a good deal to Vienna. But we do not regard such borrowings as in any way odd or remarkable; nor, if we wish to refer to the borrowing process, do we use the kind of language that Miss Margery Perham, in one of her 1961 Reith lectures, used to describe the borrowing of "Western" ideas by African nationalists:

> . . . Britain's subjects and ex-subjects have confronted her with political and, more, moral demands, which are new at least in their intensity and wide acceptance. From where, we must ask, were these new standards derived? I think we shall find that, like other weapons turned against the West, they have been purloined from the West.[21]

Leaving aside for the moment the historical adequacy of this kind of account, one is puzzled by the language. Why should the natural process whereby Africans have borrowed ethical and political ideas from Europe be described as though it were a kind of larceny? Only, I suppose, because of our residual colonial mentality, which makes us still think of Africans as somehow different—not quite entitled to borrow European concepts and values because not quite members of the European club.

Moreover, it is easy to overemphasize the extent to which such borrowing has actually taken place. How is one to judge how far a given theory, or concept, that is evidently of great significance in contemporary Africa—the idea of "freedom," "liberté," "hurriya," "uhuru," "sawaba," let us say— has in fact been borrowed, directly or indirectly, from Western sources, and how far it has been independently generated, in response to the needs and problems of a colonial situation? Social anthropologists some time ago abandoned the naïve diffusionism that was fashionable about the beginning of this century. But a form of Western-centered diffusionism seems to linger on in our attitudes to modern African political phenomena. For example, the point has been frequently made that there is a strong family resemblance between some of the dominant ideas of African radical national movements and certain ideas that occur in the works of Jean Jacques Rousseau.[22] But this does not necessarily mean that those African nationalist leaders who have asserted principles of a broadly Rousseauian type have necessarily read Rousseau, or writers of the school of Rousseau—nor even that they have been influenced, in any marked degree, by the Western revolutionary-democratic tradition. The principles that political power *ought* to be transferred from a small European ruling, and oppressing, class to the mass of the oppressed African people; that government *ought* to express the popular, or general, will; that all citizens *ought* to be regarded as of equal value and enjoy equal rights and opportunities; that, once imperialism has been abolished, brotherly relations *ought* to be established among the various peoples of the world, and, more particularly, among the African states and peoples—these principles are, clearly, in part simply a response to the fact of European supremacy.[23] It really does not require Rousseau, nor even an African interpreter of Rousseau, to convince a politically conscious African of the truth of such principles, which he (like his eighteenth-century and early nineteenth-century European prototypes) tends, naturally enough, to regard as self-evident.

Let me make clear that I am not attempting to question, or undervalue, the importance of external influences upon African social and political theories. Inevitably all beliefs are affected by other beliefs; none are entirely original, or uncontaminated. All I wish to do at this stage is to stress the element of novelty, or freshness, in African political thinking, corresponding to the element of spontaneity in their revolutions; to dispel the illusion that Western democratic ideas have been exported to Africa in the same kind of way as Western bicycles. For large masses of Africans in a variety of colonial territories to say "No" to the colonial system and "Yes" to the ideas of "freedom" and "independence" it was not an essential prerequisite that their leaders should have studied the Western political classics at Harvard, the Sorbonne, or the London School of Economics.

The "Elite-Masses" Myth

At this point I would like to question another, closely related, assumption which appears fairly frequently in Western accounts of recent and contemporary African history— what one might call the myth of "the clever elite and the dumb masses." Miss Perham, in the Reith lecture which I have already quoted, refers to African nationalist leaders as seeking "to awaken the apparently docile masses, who had not shared their experiences and who accepted the white man's rule as part of a new . . . immutable order." [24] Professor Rupert Emerson adopts at times a similar standpoint in his book, *From Empire to Nation:*

> The sovereignty of the people, even though they were largely illiterate and little aware of the complexities of the great issues with which they were confronted, was enshrined in the preambles and opening articles of the new constitutions [of the new independent states of Asia and Africa].[25]

I am not sure how much those who write in this way about "the masses," in the contemporary African context, have had the opportunity to move around among them. The airplane and the private automobile are terrible obstacles in the way of understanding the real world. My own impression is that political awareness, including awareness of "the great issues with which they are confronted," is much more widely distributed among those representatives of the masses with whom I have been personally acquainted—lorry drivers, railway workers, petty traders, bartenders, marketwomen, policemen, guitarists, Koranic teachers, Young Pioneers, and the like—than passages of this kind would seem to imply. They have usually had a pretty clear understanding of the concept of "the sovereignty of the people"—although, in asserting this principle, they might not use the language of orthodox political textbooks. True, in predominantly peasant societies, such representatives of "the masses" might be regarded as belonging to particular types of elite—comparable in certain respects, perhaps, to the *menu peuple* of the period of the French Revolution.[26] It is true also that the attitudes of the African *menu peuple* to the "great issues" of their time—to the problems involved in the struggle for national liberation —may differ in important ways from the attitudes of their leaders. They may, for example, be more willing to use methods of popular revolt than constitutional bargaining.[27] And, of course, the extent to which the *menu peuple,* and *a fortiori* the peasantry, were drawn into active participation in the national movement varied greatly from territory to territory —from Algeria, Mali, Guinea, Ghana, Tanganyika, Nyasaland, at one end of the scale, to Northern Nigeria, Sierra Leone, former French Equatorial Africa, Uganda, at the other. Nonetheless, without the mobilization, and participation, of significant sectors of "the masses"—and, in some critical situations, pressures on the national leadership to move more rapidly than it would have chosen to go—the African revolutions which we have experienced, and are experiencing, could never have occurred.[28]

"Psychoanalytic" Explanations
of African Revolution

With the abandonment of this oversimplified elite–
masses dichotomy we should abandon also the tendency to
substitute psychological for sociological categories of explanation: the common practice of attempting to account for African revolutions in terms of the "humiliations," "frustrations,"
"traumatic experiences," and consequent "pathological states
of mind"—arising from discriminatory treatment at the hands
of the European ruling class—of a handful of Western-educated nationalist leaders.[29] It is possible, of course, to apply
such methods of explanation to other revolutions in the recent
and remoter past. No doubt Cromwell, Jefferson, Robespierre,
Lenin, Gandhi, Mao Tse-Tung all underwent, at one time or
another, experiences of a comparable kind and reacted in comparable ways. No doubt, one could try to explain the rise of
Islam in terms of the Prophet Mohammed's emotional reactions to his hostile reception by the Meccan Establishment.
Indeed, this kind of thing is sometimes done.[30] But I am skep-
tical of the value of this personal, psychoanalytical approach
to history. It is not, primarily, the states of mind of individuals that need to be understood but the precise historical conditions which made it possible for these particular individuals,
with their particular standpoints and attitudes, to emerge, and
the character of the social movements in which they played a
formative part and which at the same time helped to form
them. This may sound a truism. But the special danger of this
psychoanalytical view of history, when applied to the revolutions taking place in contemporary Africa, is that it tends to
strengthen the common, but mistaken, Western view that
Africa is a special case, its revolutions unlike other revolutions in human history, its leaders unlike other national leaders, the demands of its peoples for liberty, independence, food,
land, unlike the demands of other peoples in other parts of the
world at other periods of history.[31] This is another example

of the kind of residual intellectual colonialism which we ought
by now to have outgrown.

The Importance of Africa's
Precolonial History

Let me try at this point to be a little more positive.
The basic weakness, I would suggest, of the conventional·way
in which this question of the relevance of Western ideas to
the new African states has hitherto been discussed is the lack
of an adequate frame of historical reference. I cannot supply
such a frame of reference, not only because art is long and
life (and this paper) relatively short, and because the history
of every African people, territory, and region is distinct, and
my own competence severely limited, but also because the
study of African history is still in its infancy: the essential
work is only now beginning to be done. All that I can do is
suggest a method of approach which I believe to be more valid
than the methods which I have criticized so far.

It is worth remembering at the outset that late nineteenth-century Africa, at the time of colonial partition, was
not a *tabula rasa,* an amorphous congeries of peoples living
in a social situation which we vaguely label "tribalism." [32]
(Here I differ from my predecessor in this series [F. X. Sut-
ton], who described the history of modern African "nations"
as a "history of Western intrusion"; this, surely, is much like
describing the history of the Irish nation as a history of English intrusion.) Precolonial Africa can more adequately be
thought of as a system of states, empires (such as the Ethiopian and Sokoto empires), and stateless societies, with their
established, extremely diverse forms of political organization
and approved political and moral principles. The institutions
and values of contemporary African societies cannot be understood without reference to this historical context. That is to
say, if one is interested in the question, What does a particular "modern" idea, say the idea of "freedom," mean for contemporary Algerians, Malians, Somalis, or Tanganyikans?

one must first ask, What did such an idea (in whatever language it may have been expressed) mean in the predecessor societies of the precolonial period? This, I realize, is the kind of question to which it is difficult to give a satisfactory answer. But, limiting myself to those West African states with which I am more familiar, and summarizing briefly what I have said at more length elsewhere, I would attempt to answer it on the following lines.[33]

There was a distinction, obviously, between peoples, or states, which were "free," in the sense that they were not subject to control by an external power, and peoples who were relatively "unfree," in the sense that they stood in a dependent or tributary relation to some other power. Similarly, at the level of persons, there was a distinction between "free" men and women and slaves, or serfs (though slaves also possessed certain *rights*, and in many states could rise to high office); and, within the "free" community there was, in the Sudanic states at least, a further distinction between social groups (or castes) enjoying low social status, such as butchers, tanners, smiths, and praise-singers, and those enjoying high social status, such as men of learning.[34] There was also a clear conception of "freedom" in the sense of the right to participate, through a variety of recognized channels or institutions, representatives of lineages, occupational guilds, associations of commoners, secret societies, councils of state, and the like, in the process of decision-making; and, in the last resort, the right to remove a ruler who disregarded these constitutional checks.[35] Moreover, there was the normal correlation between freedom and opportunity: a man who enjoyed office, titles, clients, wealth, was normally regarded as being relatively more "free" than one who lacked these advantages. And there was a pretty general understanding of the Aristotelian idea (not, of course, necessarily derived from that source) that the educated and reflective man, who acts according to a rational principle that he has made his own, is in a certain sense more free than the uneducated, whose virtue depends upon custom and habit. I do not even believe, as is sometimes suggested, that the conception of "freedom" in precolonial African societies was inevitably static: in the sense that the "immutability" of the social order—the principle that the liberties you now had were all that you or your children could ever hope to have—was taken for granted. After all, revolutions occurred which sought to increase the liberties of the governed, even if their official objectives were described in other terms. This point can be illustrated by the following extract from a pamphlet attributed to ᶜUthman dan Fodio, who led the *jihad* against the Hausa dynasties (in what is now Northern Nigeria) at the beginning of the nineteenth century, attacking the political practice of the ruling classes of his day:

> One of the ways of their [i.e. Hausa] government is succession to the emirate by hereditary right and by force to the exclusion of consultation. And one of the ways of their government is the building of their sovereignty upon three things —the people's persons, their honour, and their possessions; and whomsoever they wish to kill or exile or violate his honour or devour his wealth they do so in pursuit of their lusts, without any right in the *Shariᶜa*. One of the ways of their government is their imposing on the people monies [taxes] not laid down in the *Shariᶜa*. . . .[36]

This is a theme, clearly, which needs to be much more adequately explored. For the moment I would simply like to assume that modern African ideologies, like any other ideologies, need to be studied in some historical depth. From this point we can go on to consider the interaction, at the level of ideas, between "the West" and the African societies which were subjected, in varying degrees, to Western political, economic, and cultural domination during the colonial period, roughly, that is to say, from the late nineteenth to the mid-twentieth century.[37] It seems to me possible to think of this interaction as passing through five main phases. This is, I admit, a somewhat schematic way of looking at a highly complex historical process, which has taken markedly different forms in different African territories. Nonetheless, if flexibly interpreted, it may have some explanatory value.

Five Phases in Africa's Interaction with the West

During the first phase African governments and peoples—in particular those which, like Dahomey, Segu, Samory's military empire, Bornu under Rabeh Zubayr, Mahdist Sudan, were involved in organized and active resistance to European penetration—were naturally concerned to preserve their established institutions, values, and ways of life. These institutions and values cannot properly be described as "traditional," since the nineteenth century was in certain respects a revolutionary period in African history, and the regimes which resisted European aggression most effectively were in many cases either (as in the Sudan under the Mahdiyya) the products of revolutionary upheavals or (as in the case of Samory's empire) attempting to carry out policies of internal reform and modernization.[38] Moreover these regimes had already been exposed, in some instances over a long period of time, to Western influences; were accustomed to making use of Western technical, military, and diplomatic advisers; and had already modified their institutions, administrative procedures, and forms of economic and social life, in certain respects, in relation to Western models and pressures.[39]

During the second phase, after the establishment of colonial, or quasi-colonial, systems throughout the African continent, the movements of anticolonial resistance and revolt which frequently occurred—in the case of Nigeria, for example, the Brass revolt of 1895, and, at a later period, the Egba rising of 1918 and the Aba Women's revolt of 1929 —were concerned, for the most part, with the restoration of "ancient liberties." [40] Such movements were in a literal sense backward-looking, in that the rights which they sought to restore were essentially the kind of rights that had existed under the former precolonial systems.

The third phase was associated with the emergence of movements of a proto-nationalist kind—movements, that is to say, which were objectively concerned with the struggle for liberation from colonial rule, and the substitution of new forms of social and political system for the existing colonial systems, but which stated their objectives in religious rather than in secular terms.[41] To this category belong the various Messianic movements, seeking a total reconstruction of the world order, which (though particularly well documented in the case of the Congo) have existed in many parts of Africa, where either Christian or Muslim ideas have been sufficiently firmly implanted to provide the necessary conceptual framework.[42] As in Messianic movements throughout history, political thinking, during this proto-nationalist phase, was essentially Utopian. The establishment of the new world order— under the rule of the Saints, the Prophet, the "God-guided one"—would necessarily mean the ending of all forms of European domination and the enjoyment of perfect freedom by the body of African believers. It was to this basic presupposition that all criticisms of existing colonial institutions were referred, as in the following extract from one of Simon Kimbangu's "Heavenly Songs,"

> *The Whites are about to be lost on account of the earning*
>   *of money.*
> *Lord pardon them that they may be saved.*
>
> *The chiefs are about to be lost on account of their money.*
> *Lord pardon them that they may be saved.*
>
> *The police are about to be lost on account of the collecting*
>   *of taxes.*
> *Lord pardon them that they may be saved.*[43]

These movements resembled those of the second phase in that they sought to obtain, and in certain areas succeeded in obtaining, the support of "the masses." They differed from them in that they were, by their nature, forward-looking: the "kingdoms" which they sought to establish were not simply replicas, or idealized versions, of the kingdoms of the precolonial period.[44] Spiritual salvation and national liberation were regarded as two aspects of a single process, occurring in historic time, and involving a catastrophic change, which might be partly the consequence of human initiative and organization but which would require also the active cooperation of the Deity.

The characteristic of the fourth phase was the acceptance by the Western-educated urban elites of what were essentially liberal values, and their application as a standard by which to criticize and reject the presuppositions of the colonial system on the one hand and of precolonial institutions on the other. The *rights* which these elites were above all interested in asserting were the right to representative and responsible forms of government; the right of access to administrative and judicial posts; the right to enjoy civil liberties, economic and educational opportunities (with a particular emphasis, in settler territories, on *equality* of rights for Africans with local Europeans); the right to develop their own indigenous cultures; the right to construct "a new social, economic and political order such as would make their country 'rank among the civilized nations of the earth' "—indeed, very much the kind of rights in which "bourgeois" classes, in other societies at other periods of history, have been interested.[45]

It must, of course, be remembered in this connection that the process of diffusion of democratic and liberal ideas occurred very unevenly within the various African territories. In some areas, such as Egypt, Tunisia, Sierra Leone, the Gold Coast, Southern Nigeria, and the Cape, which combined relatively close contacts with Europe, the early development of a Western-educated "bourgeois" intelligentsia, and some measure of civil liberties, the process can be traced back to the first half of the nineteenth century.[46] Here the nineteenth-century exponents of liberal principles, such as Rifa'ah Rafi al-Tahtawi and Shaykh Muhammad ᶜAbdu in Egypt, Khair ed-din in Tunisia, James Africanus Horton, Edward Blyden, James Brew, and G. W. Johnston in West Africa, John Tengo Jabavu in the Cape, can be regarded as in a real sense the intellectual ancestors of the political organizations which in

the twentieth century, and particularly in the period following the First World War, most characteristically expressed
these ideas—the Wafd, Neo-Destour, the National Congress
of British West Africa, the African National Congress.[47] In
the French-speaking African territories on the other hand,
outside the *Quatre Communes,* the lack of an African bourgeoisie and of minimal civil and political liberties for the mass
of the African *sujets* effectively prevented the penetration of
liberal ideas until 1936–1937, the period of the Popular Front
Government in France.[48] In the former Belgian Congo even
more unfavorable social and political conditions persisted
until 1956–1958, and in the Portuguese territories until the
present time.[49]

The fifth phase, corresponding roughly in time with the
period since the end of the Second World War, the period
through which we are still living, has been characterized, I
would suggest, by the rise of mass national movements and
parties, which in a number of African states have achieved,
or are in process of achieving, political power.[50] One particularly interesting aspect of these parties is the way in which,
at the level of ideology, they have attempted to combine in a
new synthesis elements derived from these earlier phases of
national, and prenational, history of which I have been speaking. Unlike the liberals who preceded them, the leaders of the
mass parties do not normally regard the values expressed in
the precolonial systems that were the ancestors of the new
states as *dépassés,* irrelevant, or even somewhat disreputable.
Certain of these values, they claim—for example, the collectivist attitude to land-ownership and to the organization of
socially necessary work, or the idea that the individual defines
himself by his relationship to a multiplicity of associations,
each with its own specific functions and ceremonials—can, if
suitably reinterpreted, have a great deal of relevance to the
needs of a modern, "developing" nation.[51] This is not, of
course, to say that contemporary radical nationalists wish in
any sense to restore the forms of social and political organization that existed in the precolonial period. (This would be regarded as an essentially "tribalistic" attitude.[52]) But under-

lying concepts, like that of "African personality," which have
recently come into circulation is the notion that contemporary
Africans are essentially the products of their African past—
just as Americans are the products of their American past
and Russians of their Russian past—and that their ways of
resolving their own problems are unlikely to follow at all
closely either Western or Soviet models.

Similarly the late nineteenth- and early twentieth-cen-
tury leaders of African resistance to colonial penetration have
acquired a new importance, indeed, have in many cases taken
on the character of socially useful myths.[53] This is not because
the principles which moved them to resist colonial expansion
were at all the same as the principles expressed in modern
anticolonial movements, but because modern nationalist leaders regard themselves as in a real sense their successors—re-
asserting, in a more favorable historical context, the African
sovereignty which the resistance leaders of an earlier generation attempted, unsuccessfully, to preserve.

The Messianic theme has also a significant place in the
ideologies of the mass parties. I do not only mean that some
nationalist leaders, like Jomo Kenyatta or Kwame Nkrumah,
are regarded as Messianic or prophetic figures, though this is
also partly true. What is of greater long-term importance is
that the mass parties, like the earlier Prophet movements,
have derived much of their dynamic and popular appeal from
the fact that they too have appeared to be seeking to establish
a "new world order." They have not simply stressed the objectives of independence and constitutional change—and might
never have come to power if they had done so. They have
tended rather to present political independence as a means to
a more comprehensive kind of liberation—to the restoring of
African dignity, the abolition of colonial exploitation and
racial discrimination throughout the world, the elimination
of poverty and backwardness, the realization of peace and
human brotherhood. Part of the strength of the African revolution, as of other comparable revolutionary movements, lies
in the fact that they have succeeded in defining their ends in

universal and humanistic terms, in opposition to the particularist interests of colonial governments and *colons*.

African Revolutionary Democracy
vis-à-vis the West

It remains to consider those aspects of mass party ideologies which are most closely associated with the Western impact. It is clear that, while there have been situations in which such parties have found it appropriate to express their objectives and demands in the language of liberalism, they have been much more profoundly influenced by what I have called the revolutionary-democratic tradition in Western political thought—and, in varying degrees, by Marxism.[54] Understandably, since ideas derived from these sources have seemed more relevant to parties which have been seriously concerned to resolve the problems arising from a colonial situation, and, at a later stage, from its liquidation. Thus the central concept of "democracy" has usually been understood in its classic sense as meaning, essentially, the transfer of political and other forms of power from a small European ruling class to the mass of the African people. "The people"— the African *demos*—is usually conceived as undifferentiated, containing no significant class divisions within itself.[55] After the transfer of power the realization of "democracy" is conceived as depending primarily upon ensuring that government, which was formerly the expression of the will of an oppressing and exploiting minority, becomes an effective expression of the popular will. This can only be achieved by the instrument which has already brought about the transfer of power, the mass party and its allied organizations—trade unions, women's and youth associations, and the like.[56] These bodies are by definition democratic since through them every citizen can play a part—even if it is a relatively humble one—in the shaping of national policy. Hence the state becomes democratic once the party has reconstructed it in its own image. The

various institutions of government—cabinet, parliament, judiciary, civil service, local councils—may undergo relatively
little modification in their formal structure; but they take on
new meaning, once they become the organs through which the
party, with its allied organizations, and thus "the people,"
seek to realize their collectively agreed purposes.

This much oversimplified account should not, of course,
be taken to imply that, according to this view, an adequately
democratic system can be achieved in the period immediately
following the transfer of power and the realization of political independence. A number of factors continue to obstruct
the effective expression of the popular will: the survival of
ethnic, cultural, and economic antagonisms, individualist patterns of behavior inherited from the colonial epoch, weak-
nesses in party organization and the lack of trained and disciplined cadres, educational backwardness, the continuance of
external pressures and interferences, and so forth. The need
to overcome these obstacles as rapidly as possible is, indeed,
regarded as a further reason for equating "democracy," for
the present at least, with the institutional forms of a one-
party state.[57]

Let me return briefly to the concept of "freedom," considered in this context. While "freedom" clearly had a definite
meaning, or meanings, in precolonial societies, it is clear also
that the term has acquired a variety of new meanings which
it could not have possessed at earlier periods of African history.[58] For example, it has acquired a Pan-African connota-
tion: the idea that freedom—particularly in the sense of "freedom from colonial, or neocolonial, domination"—is a right
that should be enjoyed by all African peoples, without exception.[59] Moreover there has come to be a new insistence on the
necessary connection between "freedom" and "equality": the
principle that all citizens of a given African state should enjoy
equal rights, irrespective of race, social status, wealth, education, sex; that the talakawa (commoners), "verandah-boys,"
members of formerly inferior or servile castes, "workers and
peasants," should have access to the same basic liberties and
opportunities as representatives of formerly dominant groups

—European minorities, officially recognized chiefs, religious dignitaries, the old bourgeois intelligentsia.[60] There is a similar insistence on the relationship between "freedom" and "progress"—the idea of economic development, industrialization, educational advance, as preconditions for the enjoyment of freedom from poverty, ignorance, disease, the "tyranny of customs." This identification is based on the essentially optimistic view of history which assumes human perfectibility; since African potentialities are no different from anyone else's potentialities, Africans are as perfectible as any other section of humanity.[61] Given suitable institutions and opportunities, which can themselves be created by human effort and ingenuity, Africans are capable of producing as many outstanding and competent scientists, doctors, engineers, mathematicians, economists, historians as Russians or Americans—and will at the same time have their own special kind of contribution to make to humanity.[62] Hence the need to move forward, as rapidly as possible, from the present stage of historical development—the realization of political independence on a limited, territorial basis—to the next—the construction of larger African unions and socialist forms of economic organization.[63]

Such interpretations of "freedom," or any other political concept, cannot reasonably be regarded as "imported Western ideas"—mere borrowings from Rousseau or Condorcet. They are, rather, ways in which older conceptions of freedom have been extended and developed, as a consequence, partly, of the impact of Western ideas, but partly also of African experience during the colonial and early postcolonial periods and the lessons derived from this experience.

I do not know how far the reader is likely to find himself in sympathy with these revolutionary-democratic aspects of African political thought. Historically, no doubt, these ways of looking at society are likely to seem somewhat remote. Moreover, it is easy, particularly for those who are philosophically inclined, to point to inconsistencies and contradictions within a system of thought of this kind. It is easy also to show how often, in other historical contexts, revolutionary democrats have been defeated by foreign powers, military juntas,

or their own internal divisions and mistakes. And there is
ample evidence in contemporary Africa of the gulf between
principles and achievements—the idea of African unity and
the actual tensions and conflicts which have developed between
particular African states; the idea of the democratic mass
party and the tendency for the party leadership to transform
itself into a new ruling class. Nonetheless, I think we have to
decide where we stand in these great matters. When I am
doubtful whether my own attitude to the African revolution
may not be somewhat Utopian, I sometimes turn to Burke,
particularly to his *Reflections on the French Revolution.* This
encourages me a great deal. We are faced, surely, with clear
alternatives. Either we can say to Africans, somewhat as
Burke said to the French people in 1790, "Certainly, you can
have your revolutions, provided they go no further than our
past revolutions; and you can have your democratic states,
provided they are, as near as possible, imitations of our states.
Otherwise I discard you." Or we can say, like Tom Paine, "I
support your revolutions. Whatever your muddles or mistakes,
I believe that the historic movement which you have initiated
has a tremendous contribution to make to human liberation."
Contemporary British Burkes, of whom we have an alarming
number, try to make my flesh creep by reminding me that
revolutions have a habit of eating, not only their children,
but their sympathizers. In that case I must be content to be
eaten.

Notes

1. Elspeth Huxley, "What Future for Africa?" *Encounter,* XVI, 93
   (June 1961), 10.
2. Edward Shils, "Further observations on Mrs. Huxley," *Encounter,*
   XVII, 97, (October 1961), 46.
3. I am assuming that, so far as the West was concerned, political theory
   of a serious and systematic kind began to develop in the 5th Century
   B.C. among the pre-Socratic philosophers. See Karl Popper, *The Open
   Society and its Enemies* (1947), Vol. I.
4. The earliest known works in the Islamic tradition by West African
   authors date back to the 14th Century A.D. The earliest West African
   writer referred to by Aḥmad Baba of Timbuktu in his biographical

dictionary, *Nayl al-ibtihāj bi tatrīz al-dībāj*, is Aḥmad ibn Aḥmad ibn Abd al-raḥmān (born A.D. 1357), who is said to have written a digest of the commentary by his teacher, Ibn Marzūq, on the *Jumal fi'l-mantiq*, a compendium of logic, by al-Kaunāji (13th Century). See A. D. H. Bivar and M. Hiskett, "The Arabic Literature of Nigeria to 1804: a provisional account," *Bulletin of the School of Oriental and African Studies*, XXV (1962), 106. (According to al-Umari, Mansa Musa, the early 14th Century ruler of Mali, had composed a manual on etiquette, a copy of which he presented to the Sultan of Egypt on the occasion of his famous visit to Cairo.)

5. "He [Muhammad Bello] continued to ask several other theological questions, until I was obliged to confess myself not sufficiently versed in religious subtleties to resolve these knotty points, having always left that task to others more learned than myself." Denham, Clapperton and Oudney, *Narrative of Travels and Discoveries in Northern and Central Africa, in the years 1822, 1823, and 1824* (1826), Captain Clapperton's Narrative, pp. 82-3.

6. See J. W. Blake, *Europeans in West Africa, 1450–1560* (Hakluyt Society, 1942), particularly the letter from Duarte Pires to King Manuel of Portugal, of 20th October, 1516, quoted in Vol. I, pp. 123–4.

7. See, for example, such works of Belgian colonial apologetics as P. Ryckmans, *Dominer pour servir* (1931), or Jean Roussel, *Déontologie Coloniale* (1949).

8. Gwendolen M. Carter, *The Politics of Inequality* (1959), pp. 272–5.

9. See Roland Oliver, *Sir Harry Johnson and the Scramble for Africa* (1957); Margery Perham, *Lugard*, Vols. I and II (1956–60), and *The Diaries of Lord Lugard* (1959); William L. Langer, *The Diplomacy of Imperialism, 1890–1902* (1935), Vol. I, ch. 2; Wilhelm Dibelius, *England* (1930).

10. It will be remembered that in territories such as Algeria, Kenya, the former Belgian Congo, Northern Rhodesia, and Nyasaland, moves to abandon the policy of the forcible maintenance of colonial institutions and ideas did not begin to be made until the late 1950s or early 1960s. In Southern Rhodesia and the Portuguese territories this policy is, of course, still operative.

11. See below.

12. David Diop, "Le Temps du martyre," in Léopold Sédar Senghor, *Anthologie de la nouvelle poésie Nègre et Malgache de langue française* (1948), pp. 174–5.

13. Harold J. Laski, *The Rise of European Liberalism* (1936).

14. For early evidence of the impact of the ideas of the French Revolutionary epoch upon West Africa, see Christopher Fyfe, *History of Sierra Leone* (1962), ch. III.

15. Ottobah Cugoano, *Thoughts and Sentiments on the Evils of Slavery* (1787), pp. 25–29.

16. For example, throughout the former French West and Equatorial African territories (apart from Senegal) there were scarcely any university-educated Africans available, until about 1956, to play a part in the leadership of political organizations. Leaders were drawn, in the main, from upper-primary and secondary school graduates (in

particular, from former students of the École Normale William Ponty). See Ruth Schachter Morgenthau, *Polticial Parties in French-Speaking West Africa* (1964).

17. Kwame Nkrumah, *Autobiography* (1957), p. 45.
18. Nnamdi Azikiwe, *Political Blueprint of Nigeria* (1944), *passim.*
19. For a vigorous statement of this view, see Richard Wright's paper on "Tradition and Industrialisation" at the First International Congress of Negro Writers and Artists (Paris, Sorbonne, 19th–22nd September, 1956), published in *Présence Africaine*, nouvelle série bimestrielle, June/November 1956, pp. 356–7.
20. This seems, for example, to be implied in the article by Mrs. Elspeth Huxley from which I have quoted above.
21. Margery Perham, *The Colonial Reckoning* (1962), p. 22. I notice that in her revised edition of *The Colonial Reckoning* (Fontana Library, 1963) Miss Perham substitutes "borrowed" for "purloined"—which is better. But I still think that she pays too little attention to the antiquity of the anti-Colonial tradition and overemphasises its Western derivation. After all, the North African Donatists and Kharijists belong to this tradition also: see Charles-André Julien, *Histoire de l'Afrique du Nord* (1956), Vol. I, ch. 8; Vol. II, ch. 1.
22. See my "Note on the Language of African Nationalism" in *St. Antony's Papers*, No. X, *African Affairs*, No. 1 (ed. Kenneth Kirkwood, 1961), pp. 39–40. Cf. also Malcolm Kerr, "Arab Radical Notions of Democracy," *St. Antony's Papers*, No. XVI.
23. Just as the comparable principles asserted by revolutionary democrats in pre-1848 Europe were a response to the fact of monarchical-aristocratic-clerical supremacy. Compare the following quotation from the Declaration of Principles of the Fraternal Democrats (composed of "natives of Great Britain, France, Germany, Scandinavia, Poland, Italy, Switzerland, Hungary and other countries") "We renounce, repudiate, and condemn all hereditary inequalities and distinctions of 'caste'; consequently we regard kings, aristocracies and classes monopolizing privileges in virtue of their possession of property, as usurpers. Governments elected by and responsible to the entire people is our political creed." Quoted in E. J. Hobsbawm, *The Age of Revolution* (1962), p. 128.
24. Perham, *op. cit.*, p. 39.
25. Rupert Emerson, *From Empire to Nation* (1960), p. 227.
26. Cf. George E. Rudé, "The Outbreak of the French Revolution," *Past and Present*, No. 8 (November 1955), pp. 28–42.
27. On this point see Frantz Fanon, *Les Damnés de la Terre* (1961), particularly chapters 1 and 2.
28. Cf. Fanon, *op. cit.*, p. 87: "Mais il se trouve que les masses rurales, malgré le peu d'emprise que les partis nationalistes ont sur elles, interviennent de manière décisive soit dans le processus de maturation de la conscience nationale, soit pour relayer l'action des partis nationalistes, soit plus rarement pour se substituer purement et simplement à le sterilité de ces parties." In a number of African territories processes of the types described by Fanon have certainly occurred during revolutionary phases in the history of national movements.

29. Cf. Perham, *op. cit.*, pp. 38–9. See also J. C. Carothers, *The Psychology of Mau Mau* (1954).

30. For example, Jacques Maritain's treatment of Luther, Descartes, and Rousseau in *Three Reformers* (1932).

31. This point has been well put by James Coleman in the Introduction to his *Nigeria: Background to Nationalism* (1958), pp. 6–7.

32. J. D. Hargreaves, in the Preface to his *Prelude to the Partition of West Africa* (1963), rightly emphasises "the importance of discussing European-African relations with reference to the motivation of both sides, rather than writing as if European aims were invariably unilaterally determined, and imposed by superior technology upon more or less passive Africans." He adds that "ideally the interpreter [of European-African relations] should possess some knowledge of the traditional institutions and history of each of the many African states and peoples involved" (pp. ix–x). This may sound a modest statement of a self-evident principle, but it is still far from being universally accepted by Western historians.

33. For a somewhat fuller discussion of this question, see my paper on "The Idea of Freedom in African National Movements" in David Bidney, *The Concept of Freedom in Social Anthropology* (1963).

34. For some discussion of the class and caste structures of the states of the Western and Central Sudan, see J. S. Trimingham, *Islam in West Africa* (1959), pp. 132–7; and *History of Islam in West Africa* (1962), pp. 78–9; also M. G. Smith, *Government in Zazzau* (1960), *passim;* and D. A. Olderogge, *Zapadnyi Sudan,* v XV–XIX vv (1960).

35. For some account of the working of such institutions in the Oyo Empire and its successor states, see my *Nigerian Perspectives* (1960), pp. 137–8, 167–171, 275–9.

36. M. Hiskett, *"Kitāb al-farq:* a work on the Habe kingdoms attributed to 'Uthmān dan Fodio,' " *Bulletin of SOAS*, XIII (1960), 567.

37. Any attempt to correlate historical "periods" with chronological dates is bound, of course, to have only limited application. For example, the French occupation of Algeria began in 1830 (although it was not completed until much later in the century), whereas Morocco preserved its formal independence until 1912, Ethiopia until Mussolini's imperialist adventure in 1935–6. Similarly, the peoples of Southern Africa have not yet entered the post-colonial period. Nonetheless, in a rough-and-ready sense, these distinctions between pre-colonial, colonial and post-colonial periods can be maintained.

38. For the political system under the Mahdiyya, see P. M. Holt, *The Mahdist State in the Sudan, 1881–1898* (1958). I know of no adequate modern account of the organization of Samory Ture's state. A useful summary of the evidence is contained in an unpublished paper on this subject by Mr. Geoffrey Holden of the Institute of African Studies, University of Ghana.

39. For example, the Egba State, under the Egba United Board of Management: see Saburi O. Biobaku, *The Egba and their Neighbours* (1957), pp. 79 ff.; Nupe under King Masaba: see my *Nigerian Perspectives*, pp. 293–5; the Fante Confederation: see David Kimble, *Political History of Ghana* (1963), ch. VI.

40. For brief accounts of these revolts, see Coleman, *op. cit.*, pp. 172–4; R. L. Buell, *The Native Problem in Africa* (1928), vol. I, pp. 710–711; Margery Perham, *Native Administration in Nigeria* (1937), pp. 206–220. See also Sir John Kirk, *Report on the Disturbances at Brass*, Cmd. 7977, Africa, No. 3 (1896).

41. A summary discussion of such movements is contained in Vittorio Lanternari's *Movimenti Religiosi di libertà e di salvezza dei popoli oppressi* (1960), translated as *The Religions of the Oppressed* (1963), ch. I, "Movimenti religiosi nativisti dell' Africa." Cf. E. J. Hobsbawm, *Primitive Rebels* (1959).

42. The most penetrating discussion of Messianism in the African context is to be found in the various writings of Professor Georges Balandier, in particular his *Sociologie Actuelle de l'Afrique Noire* (1955), Part III; and "Messianismes et Nationalismes en Afrique Noire," *Cahiers Internationaux de Sociologie*, XIX (1953).

43. Quoted in Efraim Andersson, *Messianic Popular Movements in the Lower Congo* (Studia Ethnographica Upsaliensia, 1958), Appendix, p. 276.

44. For an example of such a "forward-looking" conception of the future African state, see the account of John Chilembwe and the Nyasaland Rising of 1915 in George Shepperson and Thomas Price, *Independent African* (1958). "He [Chilembwe] wanted, not the continuance of any established society which he had known, but a new African society" (p. 422).

45. See the interesting discussion of this theme in J. F. Ade Ajayi, "Nineteenth Century Origins of Nigerian Nationalism," *Journal of the Historical Society of Nigeria*, II, 1, (December 1961), 196–210.

46. For some account of the diffusion and development of such ideas in Egypt and North Africa, see Albert Hourani, *Arabic Thought in the Liberal Age, 1789–1939* (1962); for Sierra Leone, see Fyfe, *op. cit.*, for the Gold Coast, see Kimble, *Political History of Ghana;* for Nigeria, see Ajayi, *op. cit.;* for the Cape, see Edward Roux, *Time Longer than Rope* (1948), ch. VII.

47. In addition to the works referred to in note 46, see Jamal Mohammed Ahmed, *The Intellectual Origins of Egyptian Nationalism* (1960), and Charles-André Julien, *L'Afrique du Nord en Marche* (1952).

48. See Ruth Schachter Morgenthau, *op. cit.* The main external stimulus during this period came from a small number of Left-wing civil servants and teachers appointed by the Popular Front Government to posts in the African territories. But such limited advances as were made at this time were lost after the collapse of France in 1940 and the passing of AOF under the control of the Vichy Government.

49. The first political manifestoes published by African political organizations in the former Belgian Congo were the *Manifesto* of *Conscience Africaine* and ABAKO's rejoinder, *Study of the Manifesto of Conscience Africaine by the Bakongos*, both in 1956.

50. For a discussion of the concept of "mass party," see my *African Political Parties* (1961), pp. 68–75, and references cited there. There are also, of course, many African states in which parties which are in no sense mass parties have achieved political power.

51. Such views have been frequently expressed, from their differing political standpoints by, e.g., Kwame Nkrumah, Julius Nyerere, Sekou Touré, Modibo Keita, Léopold Sédar Senghor.

52. Political parties that have been loosely described as "tribal"—in the sense that they have been based, in principle or in practice, on major ethnic groupings, e.g. the Ashanti, the Baganda, the Bakongo—have tended at the same time to be "neo-traditionalist," in the sense that they have interested themselves in the preservation, or restoration, of traditional institutions and systems.

53. For example, Samory Ture in Guinea; the Mahdi, Muḥammad Aḥmad ibn 'Abdallah, in the Sudan; Sayyid Maḥammad 'Abdille Ḥasan in Somalia.

54. The whole question of the influence of Marxism on African radical nationalist thought is given inadequate attention here. Some aspects of this theme were briefly discussed in my "Note on the Language of African Nationalism" (see above, note 22). But in a number of African states and political movements there has been a considerable development in the importance attached to Marxist theory since that paper was written.

55. See, for example, the writings of Sékou Touré and Julius Nyerere. Madeira Keita, on the other hand, has expressed his view of the situation in a somewhat more cautious way: ". . . Nous disons également, si un parti politique est l'expression politique d'une classe, la classe elle-même représentant des intérêts—que nous ne pouvons evidemment affirmer que la société d'Afrique noire soit une société sans classe. Mais nous disons que la différenciation des classes en Afrique n'implique pas une diversification des intérêts et surtout une opposition des intérêts." Madeira Keita, "Le Parti Unique en Afrique," *Présence Africaine*, n.s., XXX (February–March 1960), 7.

56. On "allied organizations,". see *African Political Parties*, pp. 117–124.

57. For a discussion of the historical and social conditions which explain and justify (from the mass party's standpoint) the establishment of one-party systems, see Madeira Keita, *op. cit.;* Ruth Schachter, "Single-party systems in West Africa," *American Political Science Review* (June 1961), pp. 274–307; Martin Kilson, "Authoritarian and single-party tendencies in African Politics," *World Politics*, pp. 262–294.

58. For further discussion of some of these new meanings, see my paper on "The Idea of Freedom in African National Movements" (referred to in note 33).

59. The origins of Pan-African ideas have been discussed, sketchily, by Colin Legum in his book, *Pan-Africanism* (1962). Recent writers have rightly stressed the significance of Edward Blyden's contribution in the latter half of the 19th Century: (Robert W. July, "Nineteenth-Century Negritude: Edward W. Blyden," *Journal of African History*, Vol. V, No. I, pp. 73–86; and L. G. Gwam, "Dr. Edward Wilmot Blyden," *Ibadan*, No. 15 (March 1963). But when did Africans (including Africans of the Diaspora) begin to conceive of, and generalize about, themselves as Africans? This mode of thinking can certainly be traced back to the 18th Century: see the passage from

Ottobah Cugoano quoted above, and George Shepperson, "Ethiopianism and African Nationalism," *Phylon*, XIX (1953), 1.

60. Again, this egalitarian way of conceiving of "freedom" can certainly be traced back to the pre-colonial period. See, for example, Amadou Hampaté Bâ's interesting account of Shehu Ahmadu's rejection of the leveling reforms proposed by the *ulamā* in early-19th-Century Macina: *L'Empire Peul du Macina*, Vol. I (1955), pp. 67–8. But as an operative idea it has acquired a new significance with the rise of radical national movements.

61. The concept of human perfectibility, as developed by Condorcet and others, was made use of from the late 18th Century on as an answer to racist theories asserting the "natural inferiority" of Africans. See (Abbé) H. Grégoire, *De la Litterature des Nègres* (1808), and Philip D. Curtin, *The Image of Africa* (1964), particularly chapters 2, 9, and 10. Curtin cites the following interesting quotation from J. F. Blumenbach (1808): "There is no so-called savage nation known under the sun which has so distinguished itself by such examples of perfectibility and original capacity for scientific culture, and thereby attached itself so closely to the most civilized nations of the earth, *as the Negro.*" (p. 241).

62. The question of the character of this African contribution was well discussed by Aimé Césaire in his paper, "Culture et colonisation," at the First Congress of Negro Writers and Artists, 1956, published in *Présence Africaine*, n.s., VIII–X, (June–November 1956), 190–205.

63. See Kwame Nkrumah, *Africa Must Unite* (1963), particularly chapter 17.

Communism and the Emerging Nations

Zbigniew Brzezinski

We are living in an age in which nations are being shaped consciously and developed purposely. The era of political spontaneity is behind us. Today, social engineering as a means of effecting social change characterizes all societies, and especially the emerging nations. Accordingly, the Communist experience seems particularly pertinent to the new nations, as it involves the first modern case of a society built on the basis of certain preconceived notions held by its political elite and overtly articulated in an official ideology. The fact that these elites came to power in, and then shaped, relatively underdeveloped countries makes their experience of even more intense interest and relevance.

In a general sense, a Communist society can be said to combine the following features: It is characterized, first of all, by the centralization of all power in the hands of a disciplined and consciously organized political elite. Second, this political elite is usually committed to a revolutionary rejection of the past; it emphasizes the future, and it stresses purposeful attempts to change society on the basis of notions to which it is committed overtly and which are institutionalized in its organization. It is thus committed to a revolutionary ideological orientation, and it differs, therefore, in its essence, from traditional elites rooted in the past and usually not formally organized. Third, the Communist system is characterized by a relationship of access to and mobilization of the masses by the political elite,[1] achieved in large measure by the utilization of terror and indoctrination, both of these performing the function of breaking down the existing social structure and the intermediary social groupings, thus making possible the socialization and then, ultimately, the politicization of the citizen with the values to which the ruling elite is committed. Increasingly, with the process of industrialization, socialization and politicization are linked to the acquisition of technical skills, making the citizen capable of living in a modern society. Fourth (and this follows from the preceding), the Communist society is characterized by rapid socio-economic development, usually on the basis of intensive domestic social sacrifice and based on a belief in an industrial panacea free of all social ills. Last, the Communist society is collectivist. Collectivism in socio-economic organization and in social behavior increasingly involves self-sustaining and interlocking social control over the individual, thereby freeing the regime from some of the police functions which were so central during the earlier, "break-through" stage of development.

All of these very general features of a Communist society have a great deal of direct pertinence to the developing nations. The elites of these nations feel that they require political centralization in order to build up a homogeneous sense of national identity; that they require a revolutionary rejection of the past to build the future rapidly; that they require a direct relationship of access and mobilization of the masses, particularly since most of the pluralistic groups tend to be traditional and conservative, while the process of socialization and politicization necessitates the occasional use of both violence and purposeful indoctrination in order to prepare the citizenry for participation in a modern society. Furthermore, they strongly favor rapid development, especially since they are acutely aware of their societies' underdevelopment. Last, the new elites view the Western notion of individualism with some suspicion, since this individualism to them seems to create impediments to rapid socio-economic change and to become the buttress for traditionalism. Hence some social collectivism appears to them to be both desirable and necessary.[2]

By the same token, the West tends to reject precisely these features as incompatible with its notions of the relationship of man to society, or indeed, its notions of the nature of man. It is for this reason that there is an apparent relevance of Communism to the problems which the new and emerging nations are facing. It is this pertinence—in addition to the doctrinal-historical bias which makes the Communist leaders see the world moving in a predetermined direction—that imbues Communists with a sense of optimism that the dynamics of change in the developing nations inherently favor their cause.

It is interesting to note, in this connection, that until quite recently a voluntarist bias has characterized most of the efforts of the Communists to relate themselves to the patterns of change in what is now known as the developing parts of the world. In that sense, the Bolshevik tradition, and not the Menshevik, has been maintained, with its emphasis on the supremacy of the political over the economic; with its belief that only by gaining the commanding heights of the political system can opportunities be established for setting in motion the predetermined course of history on the basis of socio-economic trends.

Thus at the Second Congress of the Communist International in July 1920, in Moscow, where the first extensive discussion took place of the relationship between the new Soviet state and the underdeveloped parts of the world, the debate primarily concerned the strategic and tactical issues involving political matters. The Indian Communist leader who subsequently was to play a major role in the development of Indian Communism, Roy, advanced what might be called the "orthodox class line" in suggesting that a bourgeois, democratic, nationalist movement should *not* be supported in the colonial parts of the world, since this nationalist movement was striving to create a bourgeois order; hence, all efforts of the Communist movement should be dedicated toward securing proletarian leadership of the national movement, toward the creation of revolutionary situations *from the very beginning*.

Those who opposed him, particularly Lenin, argued that these tactics would condemn the Comintern to a period of prolonged inactivity. They argued that it was essential to relate the Communist movement to the national revolutionary activity in these parts of the world. As Lenin put it: "The meaning of this change is that we Communists should, and will, support bourgeois liberation movements in the colonial countries only when these movements are really revolutionary, when the representatives of these movements do not hinder us in training and organizing the peasants, and the broad masses of the exploited in a revolutionary spirit." [3] Lenin argued that it was essential and desirable that Communists relate themselves to the first stage in the progressive liberation of the colonial peoples; that they should avoid the danger of dogmatism and sectarianism which would undermine the socioeconomic basis for their activity.

This line was subsequently repudiated by Stalin, who turned, in effect, to the more orthodox line, advocated initially by Roy. With the exception of the united-front period (1935–1939), Stalin argued that it was idle to expect national bourgeois reformists to undertake genuine liberation struggles. According to him, the Communist movement should seek to create revolutionary conditions, to relate itself only to those in the emerging nations who were the *true* revolutionaries. Stalin's strategy proved to be counter-productive, and it is not an accident that shortly after Stalin's death this approach was quickly rejected.[4] Khrushchev turned to the original Leninist line arguing that it made it possible for the Soviet Union to take advantage of the assets which it now enjoyed; particularly the asset of a highly developed socio-economic system. In his view, overemphasis on purely revolutionary activity would involve a repetition of the same errors which Stalin had committed in the past.

The Concept of "National Democracy"

In keeping with this general assessment, the Soviet leadership has now developed a new theoretical framework to account for the complex problems of transition to socialism under non-Communist conditions. Their experience in Eastern

Europe, where the concept of the People's Democracy was developed to take account of a situation in which (during the initial stages) the Communist parties shared in coalition governments with bourgeois or peasant parties, may have served them in good stead. In the new and emerging nations, the Soviet leadership expected that initially the Communist parties would probably play a less significant role than was the case in Eastern Europe in 1944–1946. To cope theoretically with this phase, the concept of National Democracy was developed as a transitional stage through which such societies had to pass on the way to socialism.

In an authoritative Soviet statement, one of Khrushchev's "ideologues" defined a "national-democratic state" as one "that is consistently defending its political and economic independence and struggling against imperialism and its military blocs against military bases on its territory." [5] In his view, such a National Democracy should prepare the material basis for the gradual transition to a noncapitalist path of development; it should, whenever possible, combat the old and new forms of colonialism, and particularly of neocolonialism, which the foreign investment policies of the West were allegedly promoting; and it should be, domestically, a democracy of the "popular" type. However, its relationship with the Communist bloc, and particularly with the Soviet Union, could not yet be one based on an identity of the social order, nor on a common commitment to the same Marxist-Leninist principles. As expressed by Professor Ye. Zhukov, a leading Soviet specialist on the problems of the emerging nations, "the chief and most substantial thing that unites the socialist states and the non-socialist national states is their general anti-imperialist position—a common interest in the most rapid possible liquidation of the colonial system, in the all-around economic and cultural advancement of peoples temporarily lagging in their development, in the establishment of genuine national equality, and in lasting peace on earth." [6]

This puts primary emphasis on foreign policy rather than on commonly shared ideological considerations. Domestically, an alliance between the bourgeoisie and the Communists was desirable due to the extreme backwardness of these countries. As Zhukov put it in his statement, "For many lagging countries of Asia, and especially Africa, where the masses are preponderantly peasant, the central task in freeing themselves from the yoke of imperialism remains for a comparatively long period of time that of 'struggle not against capital but against survivals of the Middle Ages.' From this stems the possibility of the cooperation, over a longer period, of the workers, peasants, and intelligentsia of the poorly developed countries with certain bourgeois circles, with that part of the national bourgeoisie which is interested in independent political and economic development of its country and is ready to defend its independence against any encroachments by the imperialist powers. The Communists of these countries came out as selfless fighters for the interests of their peoples; they are an active patriotic force, and it is therefore no accident that they enjoy deserved respect in their countries." [7]

The Soviet view, accordingly, also rejects as "arrogant" and "sectarian" the proposition that the foregoing is not sufficiently revolutionary.[8] According to the Soviets, the doctrinaires and leftists who permit themselves to "sniff at forms of the national liberation movement that do not fit into the usual sociological patterns, forget that no 'pure' revolutionary processes take place in nature. In a national liberation anti-imperialist movement, the front of participants is naturally far broader than in a social revolution. All the more is a national liberation struggle unthinkable without that element about which Lenin spoke with regard to the social revolution —'without revolutionary outbursts by a part of the petty bourgeoisie *with all its prejudices,* without a movement of the politically unaware proletarian and semiproletarian masses against landlord, clerical, monarchist, and national oppression.' A failure to understand this diversity, an arrogant slighting of anti-imperialist actions when in certain historical conditions nonproletarian elements appear on the forestage, is the most dangerous form of sectarianism that leads to self-isolation." [9]

The Chinese Counter-Argument

It is quite clear against whom these criticisms were directed. The Communist Party of China sees its revolutionary experience as more relevant to the problems and difficulties that the underdeveloped nations are today facing. It feels that lessons from the Chinese revolution, and not new Soviet concepts, such as the one of National Demoracy, should be applied to the emerging nations. It is probably quite natural for the Communist Party of China to feel that way, since the application of a universal ideology in a specific national context tends to universalize the particularities of that national context, thereby making it extremely difficult for any ideological movement to liberate itself from its own experience.

This is precisely what has happened to the Chinese Communist Party. It has argued over and over again that, as in the Chinese case, so in the case of the emerging nations, and in recent months particularly of Africa, the liberation movement must possess the broadest social base and a mass (primarily a peasant) character. Workers, peasants, intellectuals, national bourgeoisie, in brief, people of various social strata, should join in the struggle, argue the Chinese. They note significantly that peasants comprise 90 percent of the African population (this is, of course, approximated in most of the other underdeveloped countries) and assert that without this huge peasant force there could be no national independence movement in Africa. "The war for national independence in Algeria, for instance, is basically a peasant war. . . . Extensive support by the peasants has also played a decisive role in making possible the anti-French armed struggle led by the Union of the Kamerun People to hold out for so long a period." [10] Thus the Chinese have been arguing that their own experience—the experience of a "national-liberation struggle" by the people—is relevant to all those parts of the world in which today people are struggling for national independence and national dignity.[11] Furthermore, they have gone on record warning their colleagues that "the African

people are able to discern the fraudulent tricks of the imperialists. From the historical experiences accumulated by the peoples in various Asian countries, and from their own experiences, they understand that genuine independence can be
achieved only through resolute anticolonial struggle; there is
no other way." [12]

It is interesting to note that the Chinese have emphasized particularly the experience of "various" Asian countries when addressing themselves to the emerging nations,
since the only Asian countries which have won revolutionary
struggles through armed combat are Communist China and
North Vietnam. The Chinese have also been using the Algerian experience to prove that a peasant-based uprising is
required to do the job—that, inevitably, any undertaking by
the national bourgeoisie alone is bound to be exploited by the
imperialists. In line with this, the Chinese have argued that
it is increasingly evident to all concerned that the oppressed
nations and all peoples will sooner or later revolt; that inevitably their own Chinese revolutionary experience and theories
will find an audience among these nations and peoples and go
straight to their hearts: "That is why the Chinese pamphlets
on guerrilla war are so much in demand in Asia, Africa, and
Latin America, and are considered as something precious,
even when they are no more than tattered rags, becoming
illegible as they are passed from hand to hand." [13] By the same
token, the Chinese have objected (although not quite so
openly) to the giving of economic aid by the Communist camp
to the new nations since such economic aid, in their view, actually undermines the revolutionary fervor and the revolutionary potential of the emerging peoples; not to add, of
course, the consideration that such economic aid also subtracts
from that to other Communist countries which perhaps, at
this stage, could benefit from it more.

These differences between the Soviets and the Chinese
have striking parallels to some of the debates which took place
within the Catholic missionary movement in the sixteenth and
seventeenth centuries with respect to missionary policies of
the several Catholic orders in what today would be called the

underdeveloped parts of the world. The Jesuits argued that it is essential that one should adjust to the existing socio-economic structure in China and India and utilize the existing political elites in order to make an impact. Accordingly, the Jesuits minimized direct proselytizing and tried, first of all, to establish stable relations with the elites by emphasizing science, mathematics, astrology, and not direct preaching of the faith. The Franciscans, on the other hand, argued that this is excessive reformism and that one should proselytize from the very beginning, reject the established traditions, and make a direct impact in order to revolutionize the masses, to rouse them against the existing elites, thus undermining the entire fabric of established institutions and beliefs. Time and prac-tice, however, showed the superiority of Jesuit methods; fur-thermore, the conflict was restrained by arbitration, because the movement had established practices for arbitration and an established source of authority which was recognized by the protagonists concerned.[14]

International Communism today is facing a situation in which arbitration is no longer available. The death of Stalin removed the generally accepted arbiter. Each party thus can pursue its policies in the firm conviction that its prescriptions are correct and that the other is erring. This induces, in turn, an intense competition within the incipient Communist move-ments in the underdeveloped nations. As far as can be assessed, many Communists in the underdeveloped parts of the world have been siding with the Chinese in the course of the recent Sino-Soviet dispute because of the apparent relevance of the Chinese experience which satisfies more fully their sense of urgency and frustration.

State over Ideology

On the level of state-to-state relations, however, the Soviet Union is clearly pre-eminent. The Soviet Union's policy involves not only economic aid which has been of substantial proportions, not only educational assistance, in the sense of granting large facilities to future leaders from these nations for training in the Soviet Union. It involves not only indirect "front" activity, particularly in the form of trade-union organizations; but it involves also, above all else, cultivation of the existing elites in the emerging parts of the world. In the Soviet view, like-minded Marxists are rallying toward "the path of independent development," and thus the Soviets hope that what might be called "fellow-traveler movements" will lead eventually to the establishment of organized Communist activity.[15]

However, in addressing themselves to these groups, the Soviets avoid overt references to the concept of National Democracy because this concept in itself suggests the transiency of the existing regimes and an expectation that they are merely a stage in the direction of the eventual acquisition of power by Communism. A review of the themes which the Soviet leadership emphasizes in the course of direct contacts with the leaders of the emerging nations reveals, first of all, the repeated and intensive emphasis on anti-imperialism and anticolonialism and on the association of the Soviet Union with this cause.[16] Second, the Soviets usually emphasize comparative American and Soviet production figures, in order to demonstrate the alleged superiority of the Soviet system as a vital and living concern. Third, they usually stress their scientific and technological development, especially in the Central Asian Soviet Republics, for these Republics are especially suited for establishing the relevance of the Soviet experience to the emerging nations. Finally, of course, Soviet spokesmen always stress alleged Soviet noninterference in the internal affairs of other nations as well as the association of the Soviet Union with the Casablanca Charter, and, some years earlier, with the Bandung Charter. They particularly attack neocolonialism, the Soviet term for Western economic aid to the emerging nations.

In the Soviet view this approach is much more likely to establish a direct bond with the new elites than a doctrinaire Marxist approach. The Soviet leaders take comfort from statements such as the one by U Nu, the recently deposed

Prime Minister of Burma, who asserted that "during the entire course of our struggle for freedom, capitalist and imperialist domination have been closely associated in the minds
of all of us, and it has been impossible to view the two in isolation." [17] It is the widespread character of this outlook which
makes the Soviets hopeful that their technique will be more
effective than the Chinese advocacy of more direct and radical
missionary work. The Soviets find reassurance in the fact that
what they stress seems also to be that which the leaders of the
emerging nations emphasize when they deal with the Soviets.

An examination of the speeches by Nkrumah, Sekou
Touré, Prince Sihanouk, Sukarno, Keita, and others, either
when they visit the Soviet Union or when they receive Soviet
visitors, shows a rather persistent consistency in emphasis
and priority. First of all, the Soviet Union is said to stand for
the freedom of colonial peoples; this is reiterated over and
over again in the speeches of these leaders. Second, the Soviet
Union stands for peace. Third, the Soviet Union stands for
racial equality. Fourth, the Soviet Union stands for social
progress. And fifth, the Soviet Union stands for rapid development. The emphasis by the elites of the underdeveloped nations on these points reassures the Soviets that, by avoiding
the direct revolutionary-ideological line, they reinforce the
relevance which the Soviet leaders feel their own experience
has for these new nations.[18]

Accordingly, Soviet spokesmen minimize the requirements which, in their own internal doctrinal statements, they
consider to be essential to the construction of socialism. They
rarely, if ever, refer to the necessity that power be wielded
by the Communist Party in order to build socialism—a standard, basic requirement in Soviet thinking. They rarely, if ever,
stress the importance of the class struggle in the building of
socialism. They rarely, if ever, speak of collectivization as a
requirement for the social transformation of agriculture, and
this is especially striking since the great majority of the people in the new countries are employed in agriculture and
hence, if socialism is ever to be built, the agricultural sector
will have to be reconstructed.[19]

The obvious reason for the Soviet restraint is a tactical calculation. Presumably, their hope is that the dynamic development of the situation will ultimately radicalize the prevailing conditions in these nations and that at the appropriate point it will be timely to undertake more overt forms of struggle.

However, these rationalizations for not emphasizing doctrinal definitions of the bases of socialism may be a symptom of something deeper and more serious. They seem to suggest that the Soviet leadership itself is becoming aware of the possibility that, notwithstanding the general relevance of their experience, many aspects of Soviet history have no appeal to the emerging nations. Beyond that, perhaps, the Soviet elite may even be beginning to sense that after forty-five years of "socialist construction" the process of building a new society is reaching its end and that the Soviet society is now reaching its stage of maturity. Yet it is *the process* of building a new society which establishes the relevance of Communism to the emerging nations, and not the attainment of a mature industrial society. In that sense, the Communist Chinese may be closer to the new nations, for they are in the midst of the process whereas the Soviets may be completing it.

Furthermore, in terms of internal Soviet politics, the Soviet leadership is increasingly preoccupied with the awareness of the fact that its own ideology renders obsolescent the dictatorship of the Communist Party within the Soviet Union. This dictatorship makes sense only during the process of building a new society, or earlier still, of destroying the old. In a mature society, which has the industrial-technical wherewithal for further development, the historical necessity for Communist dictatorship no longer exists even in terms of the official ideology of the regime. It may be this gnawing anxiety which prompts the soft-pedaling of the ideological aspects when dealing with the underdeveloped parts of the world. More specific and pragmatic issues may likewise be involved: the continued failures in agriculture, the inability of the collectivist model to resolve the difficulties and problems of underproductive and technologically retarded agriculture, overstaffed with redundant manpower. And it perhaps also reflects the realization that domestic orthodoxy, which might have made some political sense in the age of relative isolation, no longer can be justified in the face of global communications, perhaps even global television in the next few years, particularly to the elites of the emerging nations, elites which have been educated on the basis of fairly universal exposure to all the major centers of world thought.

All of the foregoing provides a valuable lesson to the emerging nations. It shows that the Marxist-Leninist doctrine of dictatorship breeds a permanent commitment to power, which eventually becomes rationalized artificially and produces socially disfunctional consequences of the sort which the Soviet leadership is increasingly revealing in the the course of de-Stalinization.

It is perhaps for this reason that many intellectuals of the new nations have found Walter Rostow's book, *The Stages of Economic Growth,* so attractive. In seeking a place for themselves in a broader historical perspective, they find in Rostow's book something which can justify their political role but at the same time sharply delimit it. It gives them a historical perspective which Marxism-Leninism does not offer and which Soviet experience negates by perpetuating a dictatorship after the historical function of that dictatorship has been fulfilled. Rostow's book may be good or bad economic history, but it is an excellent foundation for an ideology of transition; it gives a role and a sense of historical mission to the elites of the emerging nations and provides both a point of departure for the mission and some notion of the point at which it is concluded. This is essential if these countries are to go through a stage of development which is rapid yet does not involve a commitment to totalitarianism.[20]

Such a conscious sense of historical perspective would permit the elites of the developing nations to interact on a creative and self-assured basis both with the West and with Communism: with the West, which offers them little in terms of historical experience as a guide for the future because the West's development is not translatable into an ideology of social change; and with Communism, which seems to offer them everything, but which at the same time is increasingly embarrassed by its own past.[21]

From Absolute to Relative Ideology

Last, but not least, the Soviets, by their interaction with the emerging nations, may gradually discover—and they may be discovering it already—that Marxism-Leninism itself is inadequate as a framework for analysis of the complex phenomena of the contemporary world. Within the Communist world, the Soviet dialogue with the Yugoslavs, on the one hand, and with the Chinese, on the other, is already undermining the claim of Soviet doctrine to absolute historical insight. And abroad, the Soviet leaders are coming to realize that their own perspective on world affairs is rooted in a very specific historical experience. This experience perhaps made it possible for them to understand, in a somewhat more sophisticated way than many of us did, the contemporary problems of the industrializing societies, particularly of societies which are experiencing the first blows of modernization. But today they find it increasingly difficult to understand in a positive way the constructive aspects of economic developments in Asia and in the emerging nations, for the contemporary conditions do not correspond to those which Marx and Lenin were analyzing in the second half of the nineteenth and the beginning of the twentieth century; they find that their perspective on the world involves simplifications which they have to correct if, from an operational point of view, they are to be politically successful.

Furthermore, the Soviet leaders have already discovered that they have underestimated both the sophistication and the sensitivity of feeling of some of the elites in the new emerging nations—that they have underestimated their ability to see the world in a historical perspective and to derive from this guides to their own relations with the Communist world. The expulsion of the Soviet ambassador from Conakry in 1961 is a case in point. Another revealing example of the Soviet failure to understand this sophistication is provided by the exchange which Khrushchev had a year ago with the leader of an Egyptian parliamentary delegation to Moscow. Khrushchev addressed his guest as follows:

> If our people live under the banner of Communism better than you do, then how do you say you are against Communism. The people will tell you: "You should step down . . . we will manage our own affairs." Farouk, for example, followed a reactionary policy and used to walk with imperialism. You, the youthful officers, deposed him and this was a good and natural thing.
>
>   . . . In our country the citizens are equal. Those who want to receive education, we provide apart from free tuition, room and board. Victory will be ours, and we forge ahead and take you with us. . . . Now you do not want Communism; but never mind, we are not angry, and in the future you will see that we are right.
>
>   You, the Arabs . . . do not understand what socialism which leads to Communism is. If we view it in a practical manner, socialism is the first phase leading to Communism. You are still in your own imagination in the first stage if you want to build socialism. You are like a person learning the alphabet. . . . You are learning the "A." Socialism is the first letter in the alphabet which organizes human society, while "B" is the beginning of Communism.

The Arab visitor, outraged and insulted, replied in the following fashion:

> The observation we make to this is:
> It appears to us, Mr. Prime Minister, that the logical basis from this expression lends itself to argument, as it is a deduction based on logic. The American people on its basis, can, for example tell us: "We live under the banner of capitalism better than you do, so how is it that you advocate So-

cialism?" The American people can, on the same basis, tell the
Soviet people: "We are ahead of you in the standard of living;
then our system is better than yours." This observation rests
on the logical deductions of the statement.

We also believe that we should take into consideration in
making the comparison . . . the position of nations and their
conditions. As an example we should remember that the October Revolution has so far spent forty-three years working to
reach the present results, while the Arab revolution started
only eight years ago, and we spent most of this time facing
imperialism and standing against various types of wars
launched on us, such as the psychological, economic, and shoot-
ing wars. Yet under all these conditions, our people succeeded,
up till now, in doubling national income and producing revolutionary changes going to the roots in the manner of the distribution of income.

We should also take into account the conditions of imperialist subjugation to which Russia was not subjected before
the Revolution. Russia was one of the big powers of the
world. . . .

As to capitalism and Communism, we have not become
convinced up till now, that the historical development of man
proceeds in a blind alley, with capitalism as the starting point
and Communism as the ultimate end. . . .

All these factors make us reject capitalism not because
we hate it but because we believe it does not suit the nature,
conditions, hopes, needs and requirements of our people. This
does not mean that Communism, which proved successful in
conditions prevailing in other countries, is suitable for successful application in our country. Our people refuse to be limited
to this choice and believe that the ideological scope in the
world is bigger than this closed circle. They also believe our
people are capable, without becoming isolated from the world
wealth of ideologies, of participating creatively in adding to
this wealth.[22]

   The Soviets increasingly find their own monopoly on
socialism threatened. As the preceding citation shows, the new

nations throughout the world by and large believe that they are building "socialist societies," however loosely their concept of socialism is conceived. In this connection, the Yugoslav role has been quite significant in undermining the Soviet claim to a monopoly on the know-how of rapid "socialist" economic development. There has been a steady stream to Belgrade of visiting dignitaries from the developing nations, all hailing Yugoslavia's "rich experiences" (Shirzad of Afghanistan), its "example" (Olympio of Togo), as "a great inspiration" (Nkrumah of Ghana), its "rapid development of a socialist society" (Chona of Northern Rhodesia), its "planned economy" (Keita of Mali). The Soviet leaders, who until now have felt that their experience established a certain universally valid way of building socialism, thus face a difficult choice. If they deny that these new nations are building socialism, they cut themselves away from them and deny that relevance which they feel is the basis for their optimism and for their expectations concerning the future. But if they accept the notion that these new nations are building socialism, they contradict their own supposedly infallible ideology and their own definition of socialism. Various national forms of socialism would thus become equally valid, an idea which the Soviet leaders have been unwilling to tolerate within their own Communist bloc. In the long run, this could undermine the absolute Soviet conviction that only the Soviet understanding of socialism is universally valid. In turn, such a change could eventually involve major implications for the internal orientation of the ruling Soviet elite, not to speak of the consequent re-evaluation of its relationship with the rest of the world.

Notes

1. See W. Kornhauser, *The Politics of Mass Society* (Glencoe, Ill., 1959), for a comprehensive theoretical discussion.
2. See, for example, the very interesting study by A. O. Hirschman, "Ideologies of Economic Development in Latin America," in the volume edited by him, *Latin American Issues* (New York, 1961).
3. V. I. Lenin, *Sochineniya*, 4th edition, Vol. 31, p. 217.

4. "The 20th Congress was instrumental in helping to overcome our dogmatic views concerning the role of the national bourgeoisie. . . ." Editorial, *Narody Azii i Afriki*, no. 5, 1961.

5. B. Ponomarev, "Concerning the National Democratic State," *Kommunist*, no. 8 (May 1961).

6. Ye. Zhukov, "Significant Factor of Our Times," *Pravda*, August 26, 1960.

7. *Ibid.*

8. "The barren standpoint of the dogmatists causes them—without their wishing to do so subjectively—to objectively hamper the establishment of a united anticolonial front and thus weaken the struggle against the chief enemy, imperialism." M. Syrucek, "Peaceful Coexistence and the Struggle Against Colonialism," *Mlada Fronta*, February 22, 1962.

9. Zhukov, *op. cit.*; English translation in *Current Digest of the Soviet Press*, XII, no. 34.

   A very comprehensive statement of the long-range Soviet perspective is contained in E. M. Zhukov, "The Process of Liquidation of the Colonial System and the Tasks of Studying It," *Vestnik Akademii SSSR*, no. 2, 1961.

10. Feng Chin-tan, "The Awakening of Africa," *Peking Review*, no. 37, September 14, 1960.

11. "The Chinese people are deeply concerned with the African peoples' struggle for national independence. The Chinese and African peoples have in their histories experienced common colonialist oppression and common sufferings." *Ibid.*

12. *Ibid.*

13. *Jen-min Jih-pao*, December 10, 1961.

14. See this author's "Deviation Control: A Study in the Dynamics of Doctrinal Conflict," *The American Political Science Review*, March 1962.

15. Cf. Statement of 81 Communist Parties, December 1960.

16. Based on a thematic examination of speeches delivered by Soviet leaders to the leaders of various emerging nations.

17. Quoted from R. Emerson, *From Empire to Nation* (Cambridge, Mass., 1960), p. 483. For Latin America, Haya de La Torre has argued that "the capitalist stage must . . . unfold under the leadership of the anti-imperialist state," i.e., state control (cf. Hirschman, *op. cit.*, p. 11).

18. Some of the leaders of these new nations go even further in their statements. For example:

    "We in Africa, we hear talk about the iron curtain. We have travelled behind the iron curtain, and I can truly say—and no matter who quotes my words—that I could see no iron curtain anywhere nor have I ever felt this curtain." (Nkrumah in Albania, August 15, 1961); or

    "The frame of mind of the Soviet people differs from that of people living in the imperialist countries. . . . The Soviet people do not aim at subjecting other peoples. They have always been ready to help those who are fighting for independence, freedom and social progress. Their main purpose is to unite the world." (Mr. G. P. Malalasekera, on his retirement as Ceylonese ambassador to Moscow, June 6, 1961.)

19. This persistent embarrassment led to some further evasions on this subject at the XXII CPSU Congress. See, especially, Khrushchev's speech which somewhat watered down the requirement for rapid collectivization.

20. See the discussion by John Kautsky, *Political Change in Underdeveloped Nations* (New York, 1962), especially Chapter IV.

21. For a sophisticated African effort to put Africa's relations with the West and with the Communist camp in a broad historical perspective, see Mamadou Dia, *The African Nations and World Solidarity*, trans. Mercer Cook (New York, 1961).

22. *The Egyptian Economic and Political Review* (May-June 1961).

United States Policy toward Political Development

W. Howard Wriggins

As I was considering how I would broach the subject of United States policy toward political development, my twelve-year-old research assistant poked her head over the funny papers to tell me about *Peanuts*. On this occasion Charlie Brown and Linus were staring into a dark, star-speckled sky and Charlie Brown was saying to Linus, "Space is too large." He stretched out his hand and went on, "We really don't need all that room. Most of those planets and stars are 'way too big. The whole solar system needs readjusting." Linus said in reply, "What can we as individuals do?"

In the free world, only Americans ask "What can we do about the universe?" It is this basic American assumption that we can, in fact, do something about almost any problem that impels us to explore our role in the political development of other countries. *Peanuts* was apt also because, as we grapple with the problems of United States foreign policy, we soon come to recognize that the political firmament abroad is extraordinarily "large," and that there are very real limits to our ability to influence the course of growth abroad.

This is particularly true when we consider problems of political development, since we remain committed to the concept of national independence and the right of every people to develop their own institutions in their own way and in their own good time. We must also recognize that it is precisely in the area of political institutions that countries rightly are

The views expressed in this paper are the writer's, and do not necessarily represent official policy.

most sensitive about the role which outside countries can appropriately play.

In writing of political economy, Walter Bagehot, the brilliant British essayist and early editor of the *London Economist*, once remarked that those who would understand political economy labor under a particular handicap. "Those who are conversant with its abstractions," he wrote, "are usually without a true contact with its facts; those who are in contact with its facts have usually little sympathy with and little cognizance of its abstractions." [1]

Political development poses similar problems—practitioners and theoreticians are at a distance from each other, a fact that impedes the work of both. Being now somewhat closer to the practitioners than to the theoreticians, I can speak with some conviction about the lack of abstractions which are helpful to us as we pick our way through our daily and long-range policy problems.

One way to move toward useful abstractions is to look for ways of grouping the phenomena we are concerned with. But before I identify a number of typical situations of political development, I want to discuss several important preliminary aspects of our problem.

The World Environment Today

Our foreign policy environment is essentially revolutionary, in many senses of this term. Change is inherent, rapid, and profound. Since the beginning of man, empires have risen and declined; Toynbee was not the first to remind us of their ebb and flow. During the past fifteen years on the continents of Asia and Africa, there has been a breathtaking liquidation of vast empires. Over 600 million people have gained their independence in Asia since 1945. More recently in Africa 140 millions have achieved the same goal. Without a perception of the depth and pace of change going on outside the United States, we cannot begin to focus on the policy problems we face.

This has meant, among other things, that the responsibilities of governance have been transferred to new leaders at an unprecedented pace. One small and familiar reflection of this is the rapid growth the U.N., now twice what it was when that institution was formed less than twenty years ago.

There are other powerful and some very dangerous forces working for change and disorder in our world environment. The revolution in military technology draws countries seemingly willy-nilly into an accelerating arms race while, at least for the present, technology appears to provide a major advantage to whoever should strike the first blow. Second, there is a revolution in population growth which, in many parts of the world, threatens to engulf any progress which may be painfully achieved. Third, transportation and communications bring diverse social systems into intimate contact, accentuating friction and evoking in new countries vivid visions of how men elsewhere are privileged to live. It is these multiple revolutions which must somehow be contained or given shape by the political institutions and practices in emerging countries which are here our principal concern.

Another fundamental aspect of the world environment is that at the very time these revolutionary changes are taking place, and the old empires have been dismantled, a new, more equitable and effective mesh of relationships must be created. In considering this task, it is well to remember that, despite its gross inequities and its many other faults, the colonial order did perform certain functions. In one form or another, these functions still need doing—and many new ones press upon us.

Although the old colonial order at least kept a relative peace, the subject populations increasingly resented foreign rule. Economic ties between industrializing Europe and the colonial areas were developed. In many cases these came to be seen as exploitative. But as Western Europe goes on to a new integration, the advantages of special colonial arrangements are now more clearly visible. Although accessible only to a few, opportunities for training in modern techniques and modern values were provided within most, though not all, imperial systems. Useful procedures for settling different types of quarrels were instituted, ways of deciding the purposes and policies of government were established. Imperial arrangements also provided a protected environment for the development of modern enterprises which now have set a standard for performance by which government and private activity is in part measured.

Over-all policy, therefore, must bear in mind that some of the foundations upon which nineteenth-century world order rested are now lacking in the new order of the twentieth century. New practices and new structures must be devised to replace that old order, so that the genuine interdependence of the more-developed countries and the less-developed countries may be fruitful to both of us.

Despite the good will, the imagination, and the resources thus far devoted to development of the emerging half of the world, it is still the North Atlantic community which is becoming richer while the emerging areas fall every year further behind. The revolution of independence has not yet brought to these new countries the fruits they had hoped to reap with independence. A much harder road lies ahead of them than they expected. And in their disappointment, the easy and the tempting thing to do is to turn upon their former masters and the other developed countries and blame their growing difficulties upon us. It is even possible to argue that the time we have to deal creatively with these vast problems is running out, that history may give us but a decade more within which to deploy our imaginations and our resources to deal with these manifold problems.

United States Aims for the Emergent Nations

It is also necessary to say a few words about the interests and purposes of the United States. Priority among these values is something I do not wish to enter into here, however much each policy decision imposes a value choice upon us. Among the values we seek to achieve are these:

1. If we examine the numerous crises which have threatened the peace during the past fifteen years, the vast majority of them would be found to have occurred within the emerging countries. It is, therefore, in the interest of the United States that the emerging countries should cope effectively with their own internal problems and the difficulties they have in their relationship with one another in order that peace may be preserved.

2. We wish to preclude the absorption of new countries into the Sino-Soviet realm since, should this occur, their resources and manpower would be turned against us. To deal with this is not merely a problem of military stance, of the number and accuracy and destructive capacity of our Strategic Air Command or missiles or the posture of our conventional military forces, although these are important elements in the pursuit of this objective. Also crucial is the ability of these new nations—the countries on the Asian mainland, Africa and Latin America—to develop resilient and effective polities commanding the loyalty of their people, and to remain relatively immune to Communist-inspired insurgency or subversion.

3. We believe that our interests—and the interests of the emerging people themselves—will be served to the extent that the emerging countries are able to develop eventually more open and free societies. To meet our interest, they need not follow our formal models, but we hope that in the longer run they will design their own institutions to be compatible with ours. It is to their long-run interest, since, if they succeed in developing sound but open political societies, they need not become the prey of tyrants—homegrown or foreign. It is in our interest, too, since a worldwide ebb of the representative tide receding toward the political depths of authoritarian regimes will make it more difficult for us to deal with our own problems in the open, relatively argumentative way we prefer.

4. Although there is no assurance that a rapid pace of economic development will produce either effective, peaceful, or durable political systems, it is clear that with a rapid population growth and increasing expectations, economic progress is one prerequisite.

While we are ultimately interested in economic development because it is indispensable if politically viable systems are to be established, we are becoming increasingly aware that the ability of a country to promote its own economic growth is dependent upon profoundly political phenomena. There are a great many decisions which are nominally economic but essentially political in nature. The rates of saving, the nature of taxation systems, types and location of new investments, the approach to rural reform and increased agricultural output have important political meanings within new countries. Such decisions, when taken by governments, affect the distribution of political power, the skills which provide access to positions of influence and often affect the fortunes of individual political leaders. The principal ingredients are political quite as much as they are economic, and political development, therefore, is of concern to those interested in economic growth.

As I see it, then, our task as Americans, whether we like it or not, is to use what weight and energies we have, along with those of others, to help in the creation of viable and durable relationships to replace and improve upon the colonial order which has been dismantled. In broad terms, it must knit the more developed countries of the northern half of the world into firmer mesh with the newer countries of the south. We seek an environment abroad which is politically flexible, resilient to the thrusts of change inescapably working within it, responsive to the fundamental aspirations of its people, and capable of fending off efforts of world empire-builders to engulf it. Within individual countries, we seek to encourage the concentration of limited political and economic resources on the constructive tasks of economic and political development.

Realistic Expectations for Change

We must expect that changes will occur, sometimes
suddenly and with violence. One requirement is that these
perhaps unavoidable outbursts be held within some bounds;
they must not become the justification for international aggression by those dedicated to the righteousness of ·"wars of
liberation"; they must not become the spark for a more general war. But we must recognize that sometimes only by revolutionary change will the old holders of power be displaced,
giving way to those more able to meet the day's necessities.

A word on political variety. We Americans must be
careful to recognize that no two political societies will deal
with their problems in the same way. The manifestations of
politics in other areas of the world are sometimes very different from what they are in the United States. Political struggle
here is held within rather remarkably strict bounds by deeply
rooted institutions and by what is to foreigners a most unusual consensus concerning the rules of the political game. By
contrast, in most emerging countries, political strife cannot be
contained within deeply rooted political institutions. Conven-
tions of the constitution, what Oliver Cromwell called "that
somewhat fundamental" which is beyond the realm of dispute,
do not yet exist. In former colonial areas, the political institutions are often borrowed from abroad, for lack of indigenous
institutions fitted to the tasks of modern statehood. In areas
long independent, there are some understandings. But politics
there, too, are often acutely personal, and violent deaths for
those who rule or would enter the lists for power are all too
frequent. Affairs of state in most ages and in most climes have
previously been risky business, but men do not seem wanting
who will try their hand. Where the personal stakes of the
political game are high, personal risk imposes the temptation
to make the most of one's brief office as recompense for the
dangers.

The point is that the relatively orderly and personally

safe game of politics as it is played in Britain and the United States is alien to the wider world where consensus is lacking on the very nature of the state and its proper role, and on the rules of the political game.

As a final introductory remark, turning our attention to the constructive side, there are certain underlying functions which all political societies must perform. Governments must accumulate enough power to give thrust and direction to their activities as they maintain or generate a base of political support sufficient to ensure governmental effectiveness. While thus concentrating power and generating a base of support, a political system must also be able to accommodate major social, political, and economic changes. Institutions and practices must grow which allow a political system to cope with its fundamental problems with greater effectiveness for the short run, while working toward responsiveness of the regime to popular demands in the longer run.

It is in combining effectiveness and responsiveness that the real problem of political development can be seen, for effective government is not merely a matter of good administration. It is fundamentally a political problem, of enlisting popular support, giving populace and administrators a sense of direction, inducing at least their acquiescence and, at best, their ready cooperation. This demands the gift of leadership, the growth of institutions to define objectives and to project a vision of popular purpose, as well as a sensitivity to the needs of those outside the ruling entourage, if coercion is to be held to a minimum. In the end, durable political institutions require a readiness on the part of the ruling elite to draw new groups into participation, turning the machine of government in new directions when domestic and foreign political circumstances require it.

Six Typical Political Situations

It is easy to state in such abstract terms the major imperatives of governance. It is much more difficult to bring

these generalities into effective relationship with the hard
realities of political life. One approach is to identify a number
of characteristic political situations, each of which imposes
somewhat different imperatives upon those who would affect
events. There are many ways of turning the kaleidescope of
politics in emerging countries. The following tentative scheme
does not encompass all political systems, nor is its logic
fully symmetrical. It does not attempt to deal with the underlying variables of economic growth and of discontent which
have their roots in economic frustrations. The problems faced
by each set of leaders will, of course, be different depending
upon whether economic opportunities are expanding as rapidly as economic ambitions or whether, to the contrary, there
is growing frustration because of lack of economic opportunity. Nevertheless, as a beginning, I would like to sketch
six typical political situations.

The first, perhaps the most dramatic, and by all measures the most costly, is that of guerrilla insurgency. The second case is a situation where a long-standing tyranny is over-
thrown and a completely new combination of political power
and governmental institutions must be created. In the third
case, traditionalist oligarchies may be challenged by rising
claimants to opportunity and influence. In type four, traditional oligarchies may have been displaced and succeeded by
chronically precarious coalitions. In type five, where the military rule, the base of their political support must be broadened.
Sixth, political power may be concentrated in a broadly based
institution, as in the Indian Congress Party, or the Mexican
PRI. I shall briefly characterize each type and make a few
observations concerning United States policy.

1. *Guerrilla insurgency.* It is necessary to make a distinction at the outset between instances where guerrilla activity is virtually entirely indigenous, where the effort is designed to overthrow a tyrant, from those instances where
guerrilla forces receive support and training from across their
immediate frontier and there find sanctuary for rest and re-
groupment. In either instance, there is a combination of
(a) grievances against the government, and (b) the use of

terror and force. Those of us reared in the Anglo-American tradition are likely to underestimate the important role terror and force can be made to play if insurgent forces are determined enough and sufficiently ruthless. Conversely, we are likely to overestimate the decisiveness of "doing something about real grievances." Proper policy requires a measured combination of steps designed to deal both with genuine grievances and with terror and force consciously organized by the guerrillas.

Every such guerrilla endeavor is long and costly, for it is so much easier to disrupt the tender, fragile growth of social order than to create it that the advantages seem to be on the side of the disrupters. Our experience in Greece, Magsaysay's strategy in the Philippines, and General Templer's experience in Malaya are successful instances where Communist-organized and inspired guerrillas were properly dealt with.

In each instance at the outset, the task seemed nearly hopeless, grievances were real enough, and one skilled guerrilla could pin down perhaps fifteen times his number of regular troops. Major military and police activities of a specialized sort, designed to bring security to isolated villages and turn the tide of intelligence against the guerrillas, were necessary steps. Often, the military and police had to change their traditional role, acting no longer merely as an arm of the central government but instead becoming friends of the people against the privileged and corrupt. Governmental reforms, popularly desired administrative changes, and efforts to meet economic want together played their part. Foreigners desiring to assist must be wary of becoming the enemy of the populace. Experience in Greece and in Malaya, however, demonstrates that insurgency can be dealt with.

2. The overthrow of long-standing tyranny and the creation of new governments. We have had some experience in dealing with this situation following the defeat of Nazi Germany, the liberation of Korea from Japan, and in South Vietnam after the partition. More recently, in the Dominican Republic we have witnessed a classic case of the difficulties—

and the opportunities—of inducing the development of a reasonably broadly representative civilian regime following protracted one-man rule. The following sketch is by no means authoritative, but it may suggest some of the major issues.

After the elder Trujillo was assassinated and his son agreed to step down, several political groupings appeared, including (a) a variety of exile organizations which promptly returned to the island, (b) a broad but inchoate civilian front, (c) a tightly organized conspiratorial extremist group, in addition to (d) the remainders of Trujillo's machine, the Dominican Party. As in many analogous situations in Latin America, the military forces held the only effective power. The civilian elements then had to negotiate with one another. Economic sanctions imposed by the OAS against the elder Trujillo were continued, it being understood these would be promptly lifted once a new representative civilian government was established.

Since only Trujillo's men were experienced at governance and the other groups were divided, it was tempting to seek the virtue of continuity by retaining Trujillo's old president in power for the time being. Two brothers of Trujillo attempted a return to power but were promptly stymied by the principal military commanders and by the appearance of U.S. vessels within sight of the capital city. An Air Force General later tried his luck at a coup. The United States made known that it would not recognize this usurpation, and his military colleagues, many of them trained in the United States, failed to respond to his call, believing that the Dominican Republic already had had enough military heroes. A broadly based, civilian regime has now been established. The economic pressures have been stopped and extensive assistance is now planned. The Dominican Republic case is illustrative, but unusual. The country was peculiarly susceptible to the economic and other influences which could be brought to bear from abroad and virtually the whole Latin American community was in accord with the steps taken to replace what was a thoroughlly repugnant regime. Accusations of Yankee imperialism in this instance were notably few.

*3. A traditional oligarchy is challenged by middle class
claimants to power.* This case is more common. In many emerging countries, the leadership is relatively conservative, its
power based on land, often in alliance with the upper levels
of the army and the senior bureaucracy. During the past two
decades, there has been a remarkable movement of individuals
from the country into rapidly growing cities; educational
facilities have been extended and more modern economic and
administrative functions have given increasing opportunity
to an urban middle class. Educated young people in the bureaucracy, in the rapidly growing but underpaid communications media, young, often foreign-trained, military officers,
and, in some countries, a rapidly growing class of small busi-
nessmen share a growing frustration. They believe the ruling
groups to be over-privileged, lacking in zeal and competence
to manage affairs and standing in the way of the rising generation. Those with influence in the traditional society find it
hard to share responsibility but hang on to their prerogatives
as elders.

The new contenders for power are often more adept at
criticism than they are skilled at responsibility. Highly individ-
ualistic, they find it difficult to organize themselves for sustained and considered political activity. By contrast, it is the
men of the extreme conservative Right, long habituated to
power and still retaining control in many cases, or the men of
the extreme Left, organized within disciplined and "hard"
agitational parties with acute organizational skills who tend
to sap the will and weaken the capability of these broad center groups seeking to succeed the ruling oligarchs.

Accordingly, the policy problem is often posed in the
following way: We believe that some of these oligarchic regimes cannot long survive, even though their foreign policy
stance in the short run is more congenial to our immediate
interests than that of any likely successor. The course of
policy of their successors is always unpredictable. Since the
experienced know that only the readers of history believe that
history has few surprises, there is often a hope that perhaps
reforms can come in time. And there is often real doubt that

a capable, effective coalition of center forces can be organized to take the place of the present, narrowly based traditionalist regime. Accordingly, although we expect that should the lid be held on too tight, the whole system might blow up, it sometimes still seems prudent policy not to distrub a regime's precarious political foothold. There are other instances where it is no doubt more prudent to press the pace of change and place one's hope upon the new contenders. They may be much more moderate now than if they stay out of power for ten more years and much more ready to believe that cooperation with us is in their best interests if we do not attempt to stand in their way. We may even be able to strengthen their competence and their ability to use power responsibly by policies we adopt now.

There are, of course, a variety of approaches open to the United States. We know from experience that major transfers of economic or military resources, or technical assistance programs do tend to shore up a regime in the short run. A stabilization of commodity prices may be a basic way we can contribute to more assured levels of national and individual means. Easing of financial pressures in other ways may permit a higher standard of living, lower food prices, or improved welfare services, all of which may reduce discontent. Improved police methods are likely to permit a regime to keep its opposition, often extremist, within narrower bounds. Improving the technical competence of the bureaucracy helps provide better government services. New strains of seed may raise agricultural output and income. There are numerous countries where these immediate results of assistance are apparent.

On the other side of the coin, technical assistance and other forms of economic aid usually generate new desires; training courses produce impatience with old ways; in the military assistance field, particularly young officers are likely to take our notions of democratic and reasonably efficient rule at face value and become impatient with the ways of their elders. Well-trained bureaucrats protest at traditional forms of corruption; agriculturalists grow impatient if the fruits of improved methods go to enrich the already wealthy and leave the farmers with no more than before.

In the Alliance for Progress we are attempting to face these issues squarely. We are hoping to encourage those with a blind eye toward history to see the necessity for major social or economic changes. Economic aid will be forthcoming to ease necessary reforms and on condition that governments do all they can to forward the shared objective of development. No doubt the public repetitions of high aspiration will hurry the pace, adding new impetus to the urge for change among the less privileged. Yet it is not wise, as we have so often done in the past, to stand aside and watch pressures mount as the privileged refuse to recognize the revolutionary nature of our era.

This is no simple enterprise. There are many dilemmas within such a policy. For example, how much diplomatic friction with the government in power are we—or they—prepared to tolerate as we attempt to persuade them to adopt reforms we think necessary? How far is it legitimate to press a government to risk its own political future, if it believes the reforms or other measures we urge will lose indispensable political support at home?

4. The precarious coalition. Whereas in the previous situation, the historical problem appears to be the broadening of the political base of a traditionalist regime by encouraging it to adopt reforms, in the fourth case—the precarious coalition—the oligarchy has already been displaced and the key political problem is that of accumulating sufficient political power for effective government. New men have arisen. They are less familiar with the problems of governance, though often their technical knowledge is superior to that of their predecessors. There is a readiness to innovate; often a doctrinaire, theoretical approach to problems. The traditional ways of organizing power no longer obtain, and there is a search for new ways to structure the processes of politics. Trade unions and professional groups already are developed to an important degree. Rural movements may organize peasant demands. But these organizations are relatively new; they are not yet aware of the necessity for compromise and working collaboration toward ends they share. Very often the coalition is so balanced that economically sound and decisive policies are hard to adopt. Sometimes the balance between forces leads to the type of immobility which so weakened the Third and Fourth French Republics. If it persists, younger military groups are very likely to attempt a coup. An important element of the government's energies has to be devoted to staying in power. Great political skill is required by a leader to continue the balancing act.

On the positive side of the ledger, however, precarious coalitions are often more responsive to popular needs than their oligarchic predecessors. Mass organizations, like trade unions, grow rapidly, providing for urban workers and the lower middle class a new type of social group with which to associate themselves in efforts to protect their own interests from the harshness of early industrialization. If leadership is skilled, new energies may be released and turned to constructive tasks of internal development and a sensible approach to long-standing international quarrels.

The United States may constructively contribute by easing fiscal pressures, by devising some means for leveling off the highs and lows of international commodity prices, by assisting in the improvement of economic planning techniques and capabilities, by training programs which encourage a pragmatic way of dealing with economic and political problems, replacing the relatively doctrinaire ideas new leaders may have brought with them to power. Through exchange and other programs we may encourage the press and other media to deal with public issues more concretely and at lower temperatures, a necessity if effective political compromise is to be encouraged.

By virtue of its precariousness, only very adept political leadership can retain power under such circumstances. Such a coalition is likely to find it imperative to identify a foreign scapegoat for its troubles. There is, therefore, much talk directed against the United States, some of which is consciously designed to serve this domestic political purpose. This may be cold comfort to us, but we should take the trouble to discover whether anti-American statements represent a genuine hostility and opposition to our policies or whether they are in large measure for the political grandstands.

In this and the other instances, we have a major asset in the host of nongovernmental organizations in the United States and Western Europe. If properly encouraged and meshed in with local needs, these can assist in the development of a richly textured society where initiative need not always come from government but where skill and energy are developed in a large number of local, professional, occupational, and other organizations. Trade unions may be encouraged to be less ideological; colleges may see the virtue of a more practical, less juridical and theoretical curriculum; professional men may be encouraged to speak out responsibly on public issues and lend weight to their own experience by the independent associations they develop. In this way, skills and organizational innovations not only become part of the life of emerging countries, but also there develops a mesh of personal and common interest ties underlining our common concerns and our common destiny.

5. *Military rule.* In type five, military leaders may have seized power in efforts to bring more effective governance, to press reforms, or assert their traditional preogatives. I am excluding from consideration here those temporary military regimes which have seized power from long-standing dictators and held the ring while civilian politicians negotiated with one another and formed new governments. The more long-lived military rule is here in question.

It is one thing to seize power. It is quite another to hold power and use it with vigor and responsibility. Military regimes possess the short-run advantage of being based on an existing structure of power, hierarchically organized to get certain things done. At the outset, they are usually able to avoid the annoying compromises, the polemics, the petty or dramatic corruption and the public quarrelsomeness which has done so much to lower the repute of democratic practice in many emerging countries. Services dependent upon the public administration usually improve—the trains run on time, the streets are relatively clean, marketing is supervised and profiteers may be properly dealt with. In many instances, the military institutions are among the most modern and provide the best opportunities for technically trained, modern young men. Where the nation is beset with communal or regional differences, the army may be the most important single institution working toward melding the society into one nation.

But few polities can persist for long on the basis of command alone. The military leaders, like their civilian predecessors, must deal with subsidiary centers of power, whether they derive from traditional sources of influence, such as regional, tribal, or familial attachments, or the more modern ways of mobilizing influence through mass organizations or through indispensable economic enterprises which the leaders must enlist if they cannot coerce. Where corruption and favors are part of the tradition of office, the army rarely remains immune. The accumulation of resources possible by a coercive system should not be exaggerated. It may easily turn out that the state's growing budget for coercion and the timidity and caution their rule engenders will inhibit economic growth more than the relatively disorderly and helter-skelter civilian ways before the take-over. Nevertheless, it is possible that a puritanical military regime, endowed with the gift of inspiring support can develop a higher rate of investment than its predecessor. Yet the record would also show that most military leaders are as prone to divert resources into conspicuous investment or professional privilege as the regimes they replace.

They all have one fatal difficulty. If the military regime persists, by what steps can public office be returned to civilian hands? How can they keep in sufficient touch with popular desires to minimize the inevitable tensions between rulers and ruled? How do they loosen their hold without inducing political explosion?

Representatives from the United States can counsel moderation in the use of coercion against the populace. We can be chary of decorating an unpopular military leader. If his days are numbered and there are civilian figures likely to take his place, we should make clear our preference. If there appears to be no short-run alternative, we should attempt to direct our aid programs to strengthen productive and organizational skills among civilians, particularly toward improving the civilian bureaucracy as a counterweight to undue military power. We should work with the military rulers to direct their efforts toward civic action programs of use to the civilian economy. Military training programs should help to teach the long-run advantages under most circumstances of a military establishment freed from the onerous and thankless tasks of governance.

6. *Political power has been concentrated in a broadly based, relatively stable and inclusive political party,* with provision for fair and open elections. These political systems are relatively well-established, capable of maintaining their own internal integrity while accommodating the changes which are at work within their own societies, and are able to mobilize sufficient resources to fend off immediate threats from the outside. They are less dependent upon outsiders than any of the previous types. In part because of their relative political capacity at home they are likely to be able to play a more important role in affairs abroad. They are often examples to their fellow emerging countries.

Such political systems are better able to set the terms of their relationship with the United States than are the countries in most of the other circumstances I have described. We can ease the task of governance by the foreign exchange resources we make available, the technical and organizational skills we may be able to provide, and the receptivity we demonstrate toward their leaders and the growing middle class which tends to develop within such governmental frames.

To us it is sufficient that these emerging countries improve their capacity to remain independent and continue to organize their internal affairs so as to maintain orderly internal political processes that are responsive to indispensable domestic change. A major challenge to countries of this type is that they may become unresponsive to the winds of change precisely because the inclusive party may absorb too many men, too many interests, and too many resources, drying up the well-springs of debate and meaningful political competition.

These observations do not provide a blueprint for United States policy toward political development. They are in the nature of reflections on different aspects of our problem. They point up the variety of political situations with which we must deal.

It is presumptuous to expect that we, as Americans, can lay down a systematic line of approach to one-half of the world's people, each seeking the sinews of nationhood and the shape of institutions which will best serve their genius. However, it is of the greatest pith and moment for us to be more aware of the ways we affect the lives of others, so that in the end, when we do have a range of choice before us, we choose those steps which will best serve the common purpose of building a free world community, resilient and flexible, providing for its people greater safety and opportunity for self-realization.

Note

1. Walter Bagehot, *The Postulates of British Political Economy* (New York and London, G. P. Putnam and Sons, 1885), p. 10.

CONTRIBUTORS

Lucian W. Pye is Professor of Political Science at the Massachusetts Institute of Technology. He is the author of *Guerilla Communism in Malaya: Its Social and Political Meaning* and *Politics, Personality and Nation Building: Burma's Search for Identity*.

Francis X. Sutton has been on the staff of the Ford Foundation for several years, dealing with African and Near Eastern affairs. At present he is the Foundation's Resident Representative for East and Central Africa.

Thomas L. Hodgkin is the Director of the Institute of African Studies at the University of Ghana. His books include *Nationalism in Colonial Africa; African Political Parties;* and *Nigerian Perspectives: An Historical Anthology*.

Zbigniew Brzezinski is Professor of Public Law and Government at Columbia University and Director of the Research Institute on Communist Affairs at that institution. Among his published works are *The Permanent Purge—Politics in Soviet Totalitarianism; The Soviet Bloc: Unity and Conflict; Ideology and Power in Soviet Politics;* and *Political Power: U.S.A./U.S.S.R.* (co-author).

W. Howard Wriggins is a member of the Policy Planning Council of the Department of State. He is the author of *Ceylon: Dilemmas of a New Nation*.

J. Roland Pennock, the editor of this volume, is Chairman of the Department of Political Science at Swarthmore College.

Some Related  Spectrum Books